THE COURAGE TO ACTIVELY CARE

"I LOVED this book! These days, BBS initiatives have become like safety-award programs—more companies do them wrong than right. Scott Geller and Bob Veazie show what makes the difference."

— **Terry McSween**, Ph.D.
President and CEO, Quality Safety Edge

"Across history and people groups, storytelling has been observed as an effective method to preserve and build cultures from one generation to the next. In *The Courage to Actively Care* by Geller and Veazie, engaging storytelling is the conduit through which research-based concepts and principles are communicated to build safety cultures. The style and content of this book transcend sectors and user-groups. It can augment worker-training programs as easily as it can serve as an entertaining case-study supplement in the university classroom. It will have you reflecting on your own safety leadership "story". In a book where several notable "C" factors are highlighted, this book receives an 'A+'!"

— **Brian M. Kleiner**, Ph.D., Professor and Director, Center for Innovation in Construction Safety and Health Research, Virginia Tech

"This is the answer I've been looking for on People-Based Safety. With this book I can practically visualize the entire story as I'm reading it, as if I'm right there in the conversations. The 4 C's become more than words when I can see them in action."

— **Gary Pierce**, Process Technician, SAFE Team leader
ExxonMobil Baton Rouge Polyolefins

"This is an engaging and insightful contribution to the safety profession and an essential read for business leaders. Through artful storytelling, Geller and Veazie show that, with courage, we can confront any Actively Caring for People challenge and deliver real culture change over time."

— **Kevin Figueiredo**, Group SH&E Manager,
Woolworths Limited , Australia

"The fact that we still hurt ourselves suggests there's improvement opportunity. Knowing, teaching, demonstrating and coaching the four person-states of competence, commitment, courage and compassion, will support and nourish our culture and help provide the environment necessary for all to feel significant, valued and included. The lessons taught in *The Courage to Actively Care* will touch all facets of any organization, not just safety. I'm looking forward to learning all I can about "Actively Caring for People."

—**Michael Henry**, Safety, Health & Training Manager, McCormick and Co., Inc.

"I really liked this book. Easy to read—informative and engaging. The authors present the Actively Caring for People approach in a reader/user friendly way. Good translation of applied behavior analysis to problems of safety. The 4 C's in the model are appropriate for any leadership situation, from work to daily life."

—**Joseph R. Ferrari**, Ph.D., Professor of Psychology Vincent DePaul Distinguished Professor & Editor *Journal of Prevention & Intervention in the Community* De Paul University

"A new way to inform the world of industry has arrived in this book. Through simple but elegant and interesting storytelling, the powerful principles of Actively Caring for People are brought to light, and the difficulties of cultural perspectives that prevent safety from being a core value in many organizations are addressed, and clear-cut suggestions for change are offered. This is a must-read not only for every safety manager, but every manager, executive, and shift-worker as well. A Total Safety Culture is the product of actively caring for people, and this book demonstrates where the courage to care can be found and what it takes to correct the course of a company to a consistently safer workplace, for the right reasons— people are important, and safety should always be a primary value."

—**Chris S. Dula**, Ph.D., Professor of Psychology East Tennessee State University

"The storytelling nature of this book is genius. The concepts will ring home with many safety professionals who go through the same things day after day, and deal with the same issues and the same set of cranky managers and the same short-sighted people."

—**Gail House**, CSP, Safety Services Manager, Walt Disney World

"Having read the majority of E. Scott Geller's books and articles, I believe this is his most outstanding work. This book clearly and succinctly tells a story that many safety professionals can readily identify with. This easy-to-read and entertaining story takes all the best science that Dr. Geller has developed over the years and presents it to the reader in a simple, yet profound way. The team of Geller and Veazie hit a home run with this book. Thank you both for having the courage to write it and the willingness to share it."

— **Scott E. Barker**, Director of Safety,
Swift Transportation, Phoenix, Arizona

"I love the book! It is a quick read and delivers vital information in a way that helps the reader understand the concepts in a fun and memorable way. For instance, the little league baseball example is one of the most succinct, yet memorable ways of presenting many critical concepts in a story everyone will be able to relate to in their personal as well as professional lives. Thank you Dr. Geller for once again demonstrating your competence in explaining philosophical concepts and principles, for having the courage to write a nontraditional safety storybook, for writing compassionately about safety leaders who find themselves in your lead character's plight, and most importantly, for your lifelong commitment to improving the lives of people all over the world."

—**Chuck Pettinger**, Ph.D. , Project Change Leader, Predictive Solutions

"The ideas and concepts presented in the book *The Courage to Actively Care* are presented such that the reader does not have to be a behavior analyst or safety professional to understand and apply them. Although presented as a fictional story, *The Courage to Actively Care* personalizes the characters' experiences such that readers can easily relate and recall times when they should have stepped up and demonstrated active caring."

—**Michael F. O'Toole,** Ph.D., Director, Safety and Health,
Aggregate Industries, Rockville, Maryland

THE COURAGE TO
ACTIVELY CARE

How to Cultivate a Culture of
INTERPERSONAL COMPASSION

E. SCOTT GELLER, PH.D
BOB VEAZIE, M.B.A

NEW YORK

NASHVILLE • MELBOURNE • VANCOUVER

THE COURAGE TO ACTIVELY CARE
How to Cultivate a Culture of Interpersonal Compassion

Published in New York, New York, by Morgan James Publishing. Morgan James is a trademark of Morgan James, LLC. www.MorganJamesPublishing.com

The Morgan James Speakers Group can bring authors to your live event. For more information or to book an event visit The Morgan James Speakers Group at www.TheMorganJamesSpeakersGroup.com.

For information write:
Make-A-Difference, LLC
P. O. Box 73, Newport, Virginia 24128-0073
esgeller@vt.edu

ISBN 978-1-68350-396-5 paperback
ISBN 978-1-68350-397-2 eBook
Library of Congress Control Number: 2017900218

Cover Design by:
Rachel Lopez
www.r2cdesign.com

Interior Design by:
Bonnie Bushman
The Whole Caboodle Graphic Design

Illustrator:
George V. Wills

In an effort to support local communities, raise awareness and funds, Morgan James Publishing donates a percentage of all book sales for the life of each book to Habitat for Humanity Peninsula and Greater Williamsburg.

Get involved today! Visit
www.MorganJamesBuilds.com

Dedicated to Joanne Dean, whose lifetime of competence, commitment, compassion and courage inspired us to tell this story. As Safety Director of The Gale Construction Company for over a decade, Joanne manifested the leadership principles revealed in this book in order to actively care daily for the safety of hundreds of workers. In many ways, this is her story.

CONTENTS

FOREWORD

My ninth-grade gym teacher was the bravest man I've ever met. He was a lean Marine lieutenant in his twenties, fresh back from a tour in Vietnam. One of his arms was a short stump, amputated above the elbow. His back and legs carried shrapnel wounds so grievous he was administered last rites three times. One day he was teaching our class new rules for an indoor kickball game. My turn came to lead off for my side, and I froze, not knowing what to do. "Don't think—act!" barked the lieutenant.

My aim here is to "set the table" for the story by Dr. E. Scott Geller and Bob Veazie that follows. I want to prime you to think about competence, commitment, courage, and compassion—the "four C-words" at the heart of their story. Often we act out these characteristics without thinking. Sometimes we think and don't act, for reasons we don't understand.

When Scott, who has authored a monthly column for my magazine from 1990 until 200990, approached me about writing this Foreword, I was struck by the difficulty of defining courage and compassion. Competence can be measured and graded. Commitment can be extracted, for example, by signing Scott's "Declaration of Interdependence" to create organizational bonds among employees.

But courage and compassion are more elusive. So I e-mailed a few dozen people I know in the professional world and asked for their take on courage and compassion. I did some background reading as well.

Based on what I learned, here are ten thoughts about courage and compassion to start your wheels turning. Scott and Bob write in their epilogue, "We believe our world will be a better place when we all actively care just a little bit more." To accomplish that requires competence, commitment, and at least "a little bit" of courage and compassion.

1. *Courage and compassion are in the eyes of the beholder.* Everyone has a personal perspective on acts of courage and compassion. Bob gets out of his car to remove a trash can from the middle of the street. An act of courage? Not necessarily, particularly if the road is empty of traffic. An act of compassion, to prevent someone from hitting the trash can? Perhaps Bob's natural conscientiousness or commitment compels his act. He always picks up litter, buckles his safety belt, and helps grannies with their groceries.

2. *Waffling is OK.* A soldier from Indiana in the Civil War believed ten percent of his comrades in the Northern army were "arrant cowards," another ten percent were genuinely courageous, and the remaining eighty percent dithered between cowardice and courage. This comes from the book *The Union Soldier in Battle* by Earl J. Hess. "Good soldiers occasionally waffled toward the darker margins of courage, and then corrected themselves," Hess writes.

3. *Context counts.* The outcome of our inner struggle (Scott calls this "self-talk") —to speak out, show we care, sit silently or flee—can depend on time and place. Many emails I received from professionals regarding our ability to be courageous and compassionate came prefaced with the caveat: "Well, it depends …"

Experts call this "situational leadership" or "circumstantial leadership." General George S. Patton, Jr. described one circumstance: "Fatigue makes cowards of us all." Extreme exhaustion can put courage and compassion beyond our reach. "Running with the herd" discourages courage and compassion. Years ago in one of his columns, Scott wrote of the dangers of groupthink. "To get along, you go along" and hide behind group consensus.

4. *Personality comes into play.* Scott, in another column, described Bob Veazie waiting in the lobby of a corporation, watching a maintenance man teetering atop an eight-foot stepladder. Bob strolled over, intent on discussing what Scott called "a bothersome at-risk behavior." To change a lightbulb, the man was stretching, balancing on the toes of one foot.

Bob is a competent safety expert. He has a committed sense of duty to matters of safety. He is also quite the extrovert, as Scott noted, naturally talkative and someone who "gains energy from interacting with people," as Scott describes.

5. *Self-love can produce courage and compassion.* President John F. Kennedy wrote in his book, *Profiles in Courage*, that acts of courage and compassion occur when a man's regard for himself is so high his own self-respect demands he follow the path of courage and conscience. Kennedy wrote leaders share "above all, a deep-seated belief in themselves, their integrity, and the rightness of their cause." Similarly, Scott and Bob's story shows how people's self-esteem impacts their courage.

6. *It helps to see the bigger picture.* Feeling passionate about a "cause" draws out courage and compassion. Joshua Lawrence Chamberlain, a Northern officer in the Civil War, believed his men joined the army because they were determined to safeguard national unity, according to *The Union Soldier in Battle*.

Or as JFK wrote in *Profiles in Courage*, referring specifically to U.S. senators, "It is on national issues, on matters of conscience which challenge party and regional loyalties, that the test of courage is presented."

7. *Culture counts.* The culture, or "the way things are done around here," can either elevate or diminish feelings of courage and compassion. Scott calls this "belongingness." Hess writes in his book, "Courage itself, enshrined by American culture as a supremely valuable ideal of action and thought, was an immensely potent factor in keeping Northern soldiers on the battlefield."

8. *Life is not a battlefield.* One e-mail respondent complained: "Frankly, I'm tired of battlefield analogies to define a kind of courage most of us will never need." Scott and Bob's story describes the sort of corporate confrontation familiar to many of us. It calls for self-examination and reflection that produce moral courage to steady us through challenging circumstances, not the physical courage to dodge bullets. Many Civil War soldiers made a similar distinction. They commonly believed moral courage was a daily necessity—we've got to keep on keeping on—while physical courage was required only in emergencies, reports Hess.

9. *Idle hands may lead to lame acts.* A number of Civil War soldiers believed moral courage, based on reflection, was the more reliable form of bravery, because physical courage could be fickle, depending on emotional reactions, writes Hess. But he also describes one soldier's battleground dilemma: he had too much time to reflect. In his mind, privates, who had less responsibility than busy officers, more often fell prey to the temptation to save themselves and cut and run.

10. *Opportunity knocks, and knocks again.* As I learned in that gym class, you can blow it, fail to "do the right thing," but you will get another chance at bat. Hess writes, "No matter how badly mauled in their first battle, soldiers always had the opportunity to bounce back."

Or to quote JFK in *Profiles in Courage*: "To be courageous…requires no exceptional qualifications, no magic formula, no special combination of time, place and circumstance. It is an opportunity that sooner or later is presented to all of us."

That's what makes the story told on these pages by Scott and Bob so valuable. The lessons in leadership they teach, in real-life situations, using the "four C-words," will prepare you to "actively care for people just a little bit more."

—Dave Johnson

Editor, *Industrial Safety & Hygiene News*

PREFACE

Before there were books, people learned through interpersonal stories. Indeed, storytelling is the most common way one generation learns from another. The norms, mores, and assumptions of a culture are passed on through personal anecdotes, and the best teachers support their information with real-life events to which their students can relate. Here we tell a real-life story to teach you how to empower yourself and others to achieve higher levels of effectiveness for yourself, your work team, and your organization.

The tradition of teaching through storytelling is alive and well in today's business world, as reflected by the industry-wide distribution of such books as *The One Minute Manager* by Ken Blanchard and Spencer Johnson, *Who Moved My Cheese?* by Spencer Johnson, and *Leadership and Self-Deception* by The Arbinger Institute.

The Courage to Actively Care teaches critical principles and procedures not covered in prior fictional narratives for the business world. In particular, this book reveals practical ways to increase actively caring throughout a work culture, thereby enhancing both individual and organizational performance.

The situations and character interactions presented are based on authentic events. In fact, it's likely every reader has experienced life-changing episodes similar to those revealed in our story. The disparaging circumstances we disclose happen all too often in the business world. The solutions we offer to these human-relationship issues are founded on behavioral science, not common sense.

AN ACTIVELY CARING FOR PEOPLE (AC4P) VISION

This book can help organizations cultivate a culture of people going beyond the call of duty for the health, safety, and welfare of themselves and others. We call such discretionary behavior "actively caring for people" or AC4P behavior. Most people care, but too few act on their caring. As you follow our narrative and develop profound understanding of the psychology of leadership and actively caring, you'll discover personal power and potential.

When we actively care for someone beyond ourselves, we leap above the self-actualization level of Maslow's well-known Hierarchy of Needs and achieve self-transcendence. At this highest level of Maslow's revised hierarchy we are motivated to serve others—to actively care for people. And when we satisfy this servant-leadership need, we satisfy lower-level needs, especially self-actualization, self-esteem, and social approval.

THE PEOPLE-BASED SERIES

This book is one of four in a series of People-Based Safety books published by Coastal Training Technologies. *People-Based Safety: The Source* (2005) was the first in this series. It initiated an evolution beyond behavior-based safety (BBS)—a set of principles and procedures recognized worldwide for its science-based and effective approach to preventing workplace injuries. Next, *People-Based Patient Safety* (2007) extended and refined the People-Based principles and procedures for healthcare by explicating evidence-based techniques to prevent medical errors and sustain patient safety. The next book in this series, *Leading People-Based Safety* (2008), integrated evidence-based principles of effective leadership with interpersonal communication, peer-to-peer coaching, and culture-enriching processes designed to prevent workplace injuries and optimize organizational performance.

This fourth book in the People-Based Safety series, republished by Morgan James Publishers, shows how AC4P Principles and procedures implemented effectively for injury prevention can be applied beneficially to all other business domains of an organization, as well as to people's families and throughout their communities. *The Courage to Actively Care* explains how the metaphor of safety improvement can be used as a "Trojan Horse" to open up your entire kingdom and empower people to maximize performance at all levels of a culture.

THE COURAGE TO ACTIVELY CARE

Drs. Peter Drucker and Stephen R. Covey claim organizations need to progress to a "Knowledge-Worker Age" whereby human potential is released from a hierarchical-controlling mindset that stifles individual initiative. This reflects the courage to actively care. All the Six Sigma, all the Behavior-Based Safety and all the Customer-Focus directives will not make a difference unless people have the courage to speak up and act on behalf of the performance-improvement process. Indeed, without courage most well-intentioned initiatives become another "flavor of the month."

We acknowledge the distinct contributions of commitment and competence to human performance. But we add this third component to these ingredients of Dr. Ken Blanchard's Situational Leadership Model. More specifically, we claim people with high competence and high commitment don't necessarily apply their talents and skills to benefit people, organizations, and communities. In other words, competence and commitment are benefited by a third dimension— courage.

People need sufficient courage to step to the plate and actively care for the welfare and well-being of others. Courage is not a human trait; rather it's a person- state that varies according to certain circumstances and interpersonal interactions. This book reveals practical evidence-based factors that increase and decrease courage.

THE COMPASSION FACTOR

We initially planned to focus our book on showing how *courage* is the missing link in the popular two-factor approach to situational leadership. However, after reviewing real-world demonstrations of leadership for injury prevention and performance improvement, we realized the critical importance of another factor—compassion. In other words, those leaders most effective at bringing the best out of people are not only competent, committed, and courageous; they are also compassionate.

Over the course of history, many leaders have made a difference with notable competence, commitment, and courage. But those who left a positive legacy were also compassionate. In other words, one's mark in history can be beneficial or detrimental to human welfare, exemplified by the contrasting legacies of Mahatma Gandhi vs. Adolf Hitler. We refer to positive contributions to humanity as AC4P behavior.

Authentic and effective AC4P behavior requires courage plus compassion. A person competent and committed in situations calling for actively caring for people might not have the courage to step to the plate and act. We discuss specific person-states relevant to increasing one's propensity to show courage. But when it comes to interpersonal intervention, courage without compassion can be ineffective or even perilous.

Compassionate leaders are considerate and responsive to the feelings and circumstances of the people they direct and/or support. They listen and speak with empathy. Thus, while courage increases as a function of a person's relevant competence and commitment, the positive human impact of one's courage increases as a function of his or her compassion. The outcome is AC4P behavior. This book defines AC4P behavior as showing compassionate courage on behalf of the safety and/or welfare of others. Our story brings these concepts to life and illustrates practical ways to increase AC4P behavior throughout a culture.

IN CONCLUSION

The following list summarizes the primary learning objectives that guided our creation of this book. Specifically, after reading the real-life events of our story, you will be able to:

1. Explain why it is wrong to assume behavior is the cause of most injuries.
2. Explain why the standard behavior-based safety (BBS) program is not sufficient to address the human dynamics of injury prevention.

3. Discriminate between a behavior-based and a people-based approach to improving interpersonal performance and organizational effectiveness.

4. Integrate safety within the other key business domains of a successful company.

5. Discriminate between four critical qualities of building effective relationships and enriching a culture: competence, commitment, courage, and compassion, and explain the independent and interdependent importance of each.

6. Clarify how courage is more than competence plus commitment, and why AC4P behavior is more than courage.

7. Give operational definitions of authentic AC4P behavior and explain why these examples require courage plus compassion.

8. Define specific ways to increase the frequency and improve the quality of AC4P behavior throughout a workplace and beyond.

9. Describe five person-states that determine your propensity to perform AC4P behavior and pinpoint specific ways to increase these states within yourself and others.

10. Teach others how they can facilitate the achievement of an actively caring for people culture.

At the end of our book we provide several questions for each chapter, each designed to stimulate your personal reflection and interpersonal conversation about real-world applications of the leadership lessons revealed throughout our story. We hope you will use the questions to make these research-supported improvement strategies relevant to your life. Please start with the premise that leadership is not reserved for the select few who hold top hierarchical positions of control in the public or private sector. Rather, anyone can be a leader and help bring out the best in others, regardless of his or her position in an organization, government agency, community, or family, and thereby benefit from the teaching/learning experiences of our story characters.

We hope you enjoy learning the life-enriching principles of *The Courage to Actively Care* while you watch our story unfold. More importantly, we wish you the best in reflecting on your own behavior and becoming intentional about adding courage and compassion to the competence and commitment of your everyday experiences. The result: An enriched culture of people, empowered to increase the frequency of quality AC4P behavior and enhance human relationships and organizational effectiveness. This is AC4P culture change, fueled by Competence, Commitment, Courage, and Compassion.

E. Scott Geller, Ph.D.

Bob Veazie, M.B.A.

CHAPTER 1

"Setbacks are inevitable; Misery is a choice."
— **Stephen R. Covey**

IT DOESN'T REALLY HIT ME until I hear the "click" of my office door closing behind me. Somehow, I've managed to ride an elevator four stories and then walk across the entire floor without anyone realizing that something's wrong. I've greeted people by name, I've smiled—smiled!—and even made brief small talk as I kept moving, that was the key, keep moving, don't let 'em see, hold it together Joanne, someone made a joke, smile at 'em, yes, good, nod, open your door, get inside, close it behind you. You made it.

It hits me then. Like an avalanche. All the air leaves the room. I can't breathe. My legs are shaking. My heart is pounding, loud and fast, I'm nauseous, dizzy. My vision feels unreliable, my office looks strange, every shadow vaguely menacing. Can't breathe. Can't think. Is it some kind of attack? Is it asthma? Should I call a doctor?

I grope my way to my chair as though I'm on the pitching deck of a storm-tossed ship. I finally collapse into it, but it's not much better. If I could breathe, maybe my heart would slow down. Breathe. Deep. Again. C'mon, Joanne. You can do this. Breathe…

Slowly, very slowly, the fist around my heart unclenches. Just a little. I continue to grip the sides of my desk as though it might lurch away from me; the data charts which had made me so happy and proud just an hour earlier are now strewn across it, unimportant. I continue taking deep, slow breaths, letting them whistle out of me. I wonder again—should I call the company doctor? How's it going to look? "Safety Director Dies at Desk, Too Proud to Call for Help." Breathe. Relax.

After another moment, the worst of it seems to have passed and I'm pretty sure I've had my first bona fide panic attack. Is it possible people have these every day? How do they survive? Am I going to turn into one of them? And of course the big question: How did this happen? Who did this to me?

At one level the answer is easy: Pillar did it. Pillar the Killer. Plant Manager and Character Assassin. He's the one.

But that's the easy answer. The harder question, the real question, is "How did you let this happen, Joanne?"

Of course, the answer was simple: Some things happen whether you let them or not.

THE DAY HAD STARTED SO PERFECTLY. Cool weather for the first time in ages, so I got back from my run feeling energized instead of wrung-out. Lunches into backpacks, watch the kids get on the bus (without looking like I was watching—nothing annoys teenagers more than the idea of being watched), wake up my husband Keith, flip him for who gets the shower first (heads, I win!), out the door five minutes ahead of schedule. Joanne scores!

Superwoman can have it all, swing by the coffee shop for a Mocha Grande (I don't run every morning for nothing), and then into traffic which for once is actually moving, and on my way to the plant where I would present the amazing results of our amazing new program. Safety equals productivity, productivity equals profits, Joanne equals safety, therefore Joanne equals profit, hats off to me, Joanne Cruse, Goddess of Safety!

I even rehearse the appropriate humble-speak which a goddess must master: "Well, it's great to be part of a great team" (never mind the team thought I was crazy when I introduced this program six months ago). "Good things happen when everyone pulls together" (even though it had mostly been me pushing and no one pulling in the beginning) and so on. Winners can be humble.

Winner. I had started the day feeling like a winner.

I got to work early and was the first to the gowning room where we hold our shift-change meetings. These meetings happen daily and they're the place where one shift informs the next of critical information to hand off so everyone's clear about the status of all the process steps and equipment on the factory floor. The meeting is held in the gowning room for the sake of convenience—everyone has to be there anyway because that's where we have lockers and put on the safety glasses, hair nets and gowns that protect us from the parts and equipment we work with.

In the past, this meeting had always focused on production logistics—what parts are on the schedule, machine status, and so on. As part of the new program, I had requested that "Safety" be added as a daily touchstone—even if there was nothing in particular to discuss, it was always worth mentioning the topic, to make sure it was on everyone's mind, especially with the new program in place. The program stresses observations and peer-to-peer feedback, so the shift change was the logical place for all of us to check in with one another.

Inevitably, some observations resulted in the identification of at-risk behaviors, and that had made the entire observation component of the program a tough sell. Everyone makes mistakes, and the idea they'd have to be reporting one another when mistakes were observed had met with real resistance, even though we keep the person observed anonymous. Initially, workers felt I was asking them to turn into spies—but over several weeks of soft pressure, they began to see it is really nothing more than a form of communication designed to protect all of us. Now they willingly participate—Safety Goddess scores again.

Today's meeting began like yesterdays, and the day before, and the day before that. Presses one, six and nine still down. Why do we tolerate this? Why on earth couldn't Pillar hire another maintenance guy? (Not my department, but it seems like a no-brainer—maintenance guy costs X per month, but equipment downtime costs X times two, and the suits wonder why the workers don't always take them seriously.) We're running at a sixty-five percent utilization rate using expensive equipment, and everyone on the factory floor knows we aren't going to make our shipments and revenue forecasts at this rate. And they also know who's going to get blamed for the shortfall. I was thinking through all this as suddenly I heard the shift supervisor turn to me with, "Okay, Joanne, safety?"

"Hi everyone, OK, the fire inspector is coming on Wednesday, double check that we're ready for that, please. Also, I want to thank all of you who turned in behavioral observations last week. Your observations keep getting better and better, both in participation and in the specific quality of the observations, and it makes a real difference. I've got over 90 observations cards from this last week which I'll be putting into the system today, and when the data have been run

we're going to know that much more about where and how-to focus our efforts for injury prevention. You guys are making a huge difference to this program, and you're the reason it's working, so thank you very much for that. Do any of you have any questions or comments?"

A hand popped up. Janet Barnes, a stubby fireplug of a woman, eleven years on the floor, knows her stuff and doesn't mind letting someone know it if she thinks they are off base. "What do we know about Doug's accident on the machine-parts chute last week?" It was clearly a topic of interest, and all eyes turned to me expectantly.

"Right, thanks Janet, we need to get into that. First and most importantly, Doug's gonna be fine. Five stitches in his arm, no real long-term damage, could have been worse."

Another floor worker, Greg: "How long's he gonna be out for?"

"We're hoping just a day or two. We need to make sure his normal routine won't stretch or pull at his sutures."

Elaine, who had been on vacation last week: "What happened? He reached up into a chute, what for?"

A voice I couldn't identify: "To get a couple days off!"

Some laughter, but Janet, like a terrier, shushed them with her hand and recited the facts quickly: "The machine cycle time got upped by accident, so we had too many parts trying to get through the same small opening, and the chute got clogged. Doug reached up to try and unclog it without first locking out the power. He caught his arm on a sharp edge. What I want to know is what management says about it. Are they blaming us?"

I took a breath. Don't get baited into a management versus labor thing, keep cool. The idea of everyone being on the same team is critical. "It's not about blame, Janet," I began. "I think everyone upstairs has bought into the idea that what we want to do is make it our business to reward and encourage correct decisions, rather than simply punishing bad ones. No one is in trouble, we just need to know what happened, and we also need to look at how the machine cycle got bumped up."

Janet looked incredulous. "We know how the cycle got bumped up, Joanne, it's because we have so many machines down because we don't have enough maintenance people. And the machines are so old that the replacement parts are impossible to find, and so any machine that's lucky enough to still be working has to work twice as fast, and meanwhile we're getting leaned on all day every day about customers complaining about late orders. Why are we so slow, yada-yada-yada? We unclog parts like this in machine exit-chutes all the time. We're being pushed to cut corners. That's the observation I'd like to submit today."

A murmur of agreement. Expectant faces turned my way to see how I would react to this second attempt to bait me into an us-versus-them discussion. What Janet doesn't want to believe is that I'm really on her side, and the side of everyone working on that floor.

"I have our weekly BBS Steering Committee in twenty minutes Janet, and you had better believe this problem is at the very top of my list. We've got to find a way to relieve the pressure on you folks, because you're too valuable to be kept in this kind of situation. But you need to understand that part of how I make that argument is by being able to show everything we're doing right, and that includes chasing down the contributing factors of every incident and doing whatever we can to fix things when they go wrong. For instance, no matter what the machine cycle was, we know Doug should have locked out the power before reaching up into the chute. So let's double check that we're all clear about those procedures."

The next ten minutes were spent discussing the location of the controls for machine speed, access to the controls, whether they could be housed more protectively, whether a key should be required, and so on. My committee meeting was looming, so I cut it short, summing up: "These are all good ideas, we're gonna look at everything. But what's important is for all of you to understand— you're doing great, we've got very high participation in the BBS process, up twenty percent in two months, all our numbers are better than I expected, so, let me say it again: No one is in any trouble."

"No one is in any trouble." I had actually said that.

I made a quick round of goodbyes and headed to the Steering Committee Meeting. As I entered the admin building, my stomach is starting to flutter, and I wondered whether that Mocha Grande had been too much caffeine for an already nervous day. Oh well, I thought—at least it will keep me awake.

If you were to ask any of the people actually working the floor at the plant what goes on in the admin building, the odds are they'd roll their eyes and say, "They're having a meeting to schedule their next five meetings." It's more than a little bit true, but I made my peace with the coat-and-tie crowd long ago. We don't just manufacture, we also market and sell and pay bills and manage retirement plans and dozens of other tasks. Unless you want twenty horses pulling in twenty different directions, you're going to have to sit down and talk every now and then. And this meeting was more or less my baby because it dealt specifically with the BBS processes I had pushed for, and my progress report would be the high point. This was the moment I had been gearing up for all week. I couldn't wait!

But of course, meetings are about waiting. We had a full agenda. Start with a review of the Doug Sloan incident, schedule future observer training, decide on next steps of process improvement, and only then would I give my progress report…and I expected at that point we'd want to discuss celebrating our current successes.

We got through the agenda items I thought of as the prelim, and then I had the floor. I began by sharing the participation charts, which highlighted the overall growth and acceptance of the BBS program by the workers at large. We'd had several discussions about how best to achieve these kinds of numbers, and the fact that we had succeeded drew a very gratifying round of applause, and sure enough, there was an immediate suggestion that some sort of celebration was in order. I couldn't have been happier, not only because our successes were so clear but also because the shift-change meeting was still fresh in my mind, and I knew a celebration would be good for morale on the floor.

I should have known that even the most worthy topic can start to feel like a lecture on quantum mechanics when enough people weigh in. Before I knew it, we found ourselves in one of "those" meetings, in which I watched almost eight man hours being devoured by what is essentially party planning. How about a Mexican theme? Yes, but what if someone found it offensive? Are tacos inherently offensive? (I hereby swear on a stack of Bibles we spent almost ten minutes on that question.) What about a mini carnival with a dunking tank? Maybe Joanne could be the target! (Hardy harhar said I, following with a firm veto into the laughing faces.)

At last, we settled on an extended afternoon break with an ice cream sundae bar—lots of flavors and toppings, a non-fat yogurt for anyone counting calories, all in favor, resounding "Ayes!" and thank heavens, that's done. I knew the workers would enjoy the ice cream and appreciate the gesture, but as I rose to leave the meeting, I imagined how the folks in the plant would giggle if they knew how long this monumental decision had taken.

I was almost through the door when from behind me I heard "Hey Joanne, should we maybe get Bob Pillar to say something?"

This was a good idea. Bob Pillar is the General Manager of the plant, and he is widely known as a tough man to please. But, me, the "Safety Goddess"—I can get anything. "I'll give him a call and let him know I think a few words from him to the workers would be a smart move."

I felt a little thrill of power at the notion little old me might simply "mention" something to Pillar the Killer as "a smart move" and he would instantly leap into action on my say-so. I could actually feel my status in the room go up as I implied this casual authority: Bob? My good pal, Bob? Oh sure, I'll have him speak to the troops, no worries.

As I moved away from the conference room I bumped into Roger Kingsley, one of our most senior press operators and one of the folks I value most among the plant workers. He is good humored, practical, and has been here so long he has already forgotten more company history than most of us will ever know. I smiled at him. "Hi ya, Roger, seeing how the other half lives?"

He grinned back at me and held up a cup of coffee. "Ya caught me. They have better coffee here than we have on the snack truck."

"I won't tell. Hey, I just got out of our BBS Steering Committee meeting and we're the talk of the town."

His eyebrows rose, "That right?"

I nodded enthusiastically, "Absolutely. When I showed them we had gone from forty percent participation to almost eighty-five, you would've thought I had told them we just landed on Jupiter. That kind of buy-in seemed like a pipe dream just a few months ago."

Roger shrugged. "Look, you know I was as skeptical as anyone else. I didn't like the idea of me watching everyone and everyone watching me. But after a while, you see that it makes sense, it starts to feel like we're looking out for each other, not just watching each other. You know, two of those BOPs are mine."

He is talking about the Behavior Observation Process (BOP) cards, and nothing pleased me more than knowing such a senior worker is on board with me. Plenty of times the older workers are the most resistant to change, but Roger doesn't care whether an idea is old or new, as long as it works. This is part of what makes him such a good guy to have around, and I always take whatever he says very seriously, which is why his next comment caught my attention: "I gotta say though, I'm not sure a big stack of cards is necessarily good news all by itself."

"Why not?"

"Well, you know how it is down there. There's always some new program, right? And so when you or some manager says 'You gotta do this now' we'll do it, but we don't always really do it, you know. I bet if you looked through all your cards, you'd find plenty with only check-marks, and no comments about hazards or feedback or anything else. This doesn't really tell you much except they know how to fill out a BOP card really fast."

I tried a glass-half-full approach. "I hear you, but hey—three months ago, they weren't even filling out the cards. Let's do this—how about at our next Steering Committee meeting we bring this up, you and I together, and we see if we can nudge people up to that next level. Because you're right, the more they tell us, the better we can make things. What do you think?"

He grinned again. "That's why you get the big bucks, Jo—always thinking ahead." Saluting me with his coffee, he moved along.

I got back to my office, reflecting on how lucky I am to have people like Roger backing me up as we move forward bit by bit. I sorted through some messages, including one from our external safety consultant, congratulating me on our progress and letting me know he is available to help us reach "the next level." The phone chirped and I picked it up, "Joanne Cruse."

An impossibly cheerful voice on the other end, "Hi, Ms. Cruse, this is Becky from US Cell, I wonder if you have a minute to talk about your account?"

I smiled to myself. This would be fun. I kept my voice grave. "You're calling because I haven't paid my last bill."

"Well, you are a valued customer, and so we are concerned that something might be wrong."

"I'm not a valued customer."

An uncomfortable pause. Poor Becky was having a bad Monday morning. "Well, um, if you could…"

"I'm sure you have my account on your screen in front of you, how much would you say I pay per month, roughly, on average?"

Becky's voice moved from cheerful to cautious. "Well…it looks like a little under three hundred dollars?"

"That's right; now tell me this, Becky, does that seem odd to you?"

Uh oh. Another deviation from her script. The poor thing. "Well, I'm not sure wha—"

"I mean, you go after new customers by offering them terrific plans that cost about a quarter of what I'm paying, and I've been with you for over ten years, so what I'm curious about is why you give strangers better deals than you give me if I'm such a valued customer."

Becky's train had totally jumped the tracks now. I could hear papers rustling and I imagined the poor girl's sweat as she struggled to maintain some form of friendly assistance. "Well, I'm sure we could find you some—"

"Becky," I interrupted her gently. "They aren't paying you enough to pretend they're good guys when all they care about is more customers and more profit, and I know it's not your own personal fault that no one has ever called me to check how I'm doing…but when your bosses ask you why I cancelled my account, you tell them it's because they didn't care. I know they say they care, but caring is a verb, it's active, you have to do something when you care, and they missed their chance. I'll mail my last check this week, and I hope they don't make you do too many more of these calls, Becky. Have a nice day." Score one for the tiny consumer. Score another win for me.

My phone chirped again and I answered, rolling my eyes. "Becky, I promise you, there's nothing more for us to discuss."

A pause in which I imagined a twenty-something girl trying to think of a convincing apology…and then a gruff male voice: "Joanne?"

Uh oh. "I'm sorry, yes, this is Joanne Cruse?"

"It's Bob Pillar. I need to see you as soon as you've got a minute."

I nearly gave myself whiplash recoiling from the phone. Bob Pillar the GM calling me and I answer the phone like I'm in some sorority! I struggled for my businesswoman's voice. "Hi Mr. Pillar, sorry, I grabbed the wrong line, you'd like me to come up to your office?"

"As soon as you can, thank you." And he's gone.

Weird. Spooky even. Bob Pillar isn't just a tough man to please; he is someone who keeps his interactions with lower staff to a bare minimum. It's rumored the top executives and board members love him, but the folks beneath him don't know enough about him to do much except worry whenever he comes onto their radar. And now he had summoned me, with all of the cool terseness of a general commanding a private to pick up his dry cleaning.

Well, so be it. This wasn't a crisis, it was an opportunity! I could give him the same report I had given the Steering Committee, and I could also lobby him to come to the ice cream social. His calling me at this moment was nothing more than good luck. The Safety Goddess scores again!

CHAPTER 2

"Adversity is the first path to truth."
— **Lord Byron**

S TILL BRIMMING WITH OPTIMISM, I took the elevator up to the top floor of the admin building. As I walked down the corridor, I passed the Wall of Fame which seems an obligatory segment en route to any executive's office. Here were the blown-up reprints of newspaper and magazine articles, there were the plaques and certificates, all of it vaguely desperate in its aspirations to impress.

At the end, the worst of the bunch, a small selection of photos commemorating the visits of various smiling VIP's whom I always privately thought of as SIP's (Semi-Important Persons). I mean come on—the Lieutenant

Governor from 1988? Robert Goulet? I almost always caught myself smiling and then struggling to hide it as the Wall of Fame played out and I entered the outer office, dominated by a large semi-circular desk behind which sat Barbara St. Claire, Bob Pillar's personal secretary.

Barbara is a bit of a cipher to the rest of us at the plant. Of course she's of interest because she is the gatekeeper between the boss and the rest of the world, and there are a range of assessments of her. She's certainly attractive, and so there are the usual schoolyard speculations about her "duties," but her behavior never seems the least bit flirtatious. She dresses conservatively, her hair is always back, and her age is difficult to place—a mature thirty? A very fit fifty? She seems to know everyone's name, and always wears a pleasant smile which somehow never quite reaches her eyes. In my mind, she's the perfect extension of Pillar—cool, distant, businesslike, and just a little bit intimidating.

Her impersonal smile flashed as she caught sight of me. "Hi Joanne," she said. "Mr. Pillar had to take a call from the Canadian plant, he'll only be a minute. Can I get you anything?"

Even in that tiny exchange, a wealth of information. "Mr. Pillar" always, never "Bob." Her immediate recognition of me, her familiar use of my name. Her offer of "anything" although she never twitched a muscle to get up and there was never any evidence of coffee, or any other refreshments for that matter. Maybe they didn't need food or drink up here.

I did my best to return her cool smile. "Thanks, Barbara, I'm fine, I'll just have a seat." (You betcha, I thought, I'll tell you what I'll be doing—I'm the Director of Safety, for goodness sake!)

I settled into one of the two seats along the wall, and pretended to go over the notes I had brought. I didn't actually need to look at them, I practically had them memorized, but I wasn't about to seem idle while in Barbara's gaze. Why was I so nervous? It's not as though I was there to be interviewed for some entry-level job. I was a key staff member who came bearing good news of hard-won success!

This train of thought helped the muscles unclench a little, and I followed it a bit further. Pillar must have heard how well things are going, and he wants to discuss it personally with me. And I've got the graphs and charts right here to help him see exactly how far we've come. The program I had initiated had been an instant success. New safety programs seem to come along annually, and they're often little more than last year's program dressed up in new language. But BBS is different.

BBS stands for Behavior-Based Safety, which evolved from much published behavioral science research. Traditionally, safety programs have tried different tactics for reminding people to be safe. An idea is planted, and repeated, with hopes that repetition of the idea will lead to the workers' behavior changing and becoming more safe. It's an inside-out strategy: if the person's insides—the thoughts, the attitude—can be changed, then the relevant behavior will follow and safer work practices will result.

The traditional approach is certainly better than nothing, and various versions of it have achieved some success over the years. The introduction of BBS programs in the mid-1980s stood everything on its head. BBS starts from the assumption behavior can be changed from the outside in, that workers trained to observe each other's behavior will help each other improve their behavior. In BBS programs, workers observe each other, give each other behavior-based feedback, and submit written reports of their observations (the cards Roger and I had talked about earlier are one example). In the old model, workers were trained en masse, almost like cattle, on the safety policies and regulations. Then supervisors were supposed to act like safety cops and enforce the rules.

In a BBS program, workers feel a true sense of ownership. It's our program, we're the ones who make the observations and identify the risks and the fixes. Initially there's some suspicion, because we feel we're being asked to spy on one another. It doesn't take long, though, for us to begin to understand we're working as a team, and there's a big difference between spying on each other and taking care of each other.

In a successful BBS environment, there's a real sense of collaboration and shared goals, and as the injuries decrease in both severity and frequency, we feel our successes, which leads to still greater participation and greater results. It's a feedback loop, reinforcing itself with every iteration, growing and strengthening to everyone's benefit.

I had spent several weeks last year convincing the top brass to spend the money to bring in the top BBS consulting firm to help us implement this evidence-based approach. And now, three months into the year, we had demonstrated significant growth and improvement in all areas, achieving eighty-five percent active participation from the plant's entire workforce. Our benchmark for this month had been seventy percent and that's one reason I am so thrilled. We've exceeded every measurable goal so far, and there was no reason to think we couldn't continue.

I held these thoughts close as the speaker on Barbara's desk buzzed and Pillar's voice came through with a brusque, "Send her in."

His tone made me waver, and I struggled to maintain my poise. Ignore the curtness of his voice. He was speaking to his assistant, not to me. He was a busy man with a lot on his mind. I was about to make his day. I rose smoothly and moved toward his office smiling a "Thanks, Barbara," toward the desk, letting her know I didn't need the gatekeeper to tell me what I already knew—I was expected, and Bob and I were both busy people who didn't have time to waste. I knew my casual dismissal of her was petty, and that didn't make it one bit less entertaining. I wasn't some schoolgirl sent to the principal's office. I was an important person bearing important news.

I closed the door behind me and took a beat to locate Bob behind his desk and to assess his mood.

The room felt chilly, and I was pretty sure it had nothing to do with air conditioning. Part of it was certainly the décor, or rather the lack thereof. Bob Pillar's office is as no-nonsense as the man himself, and there are Super-8 Motel rooms decorated with a better sense of style. His desk was clear except for a few folders, no knickknacks, no family photos.

The walls were devoid of anything decorative beyond a seascape lithograph of the ten-for-ten-bucks variety found in shopping mall parking lots…and there, quietly, behind his desk, five years' worth of Gold Performance Awards. Their arrangement on the wall left the impression he had every expectation of adding number six soon, and I recalled that this year's emphasis on linking performance awards to safety had been a big factor in my persuading them to move forward with the BBS program.

Bob himself was behind his desk, turned to one side, studying an old CRT monitor angled to prevent easy sight of his face. No high-tech, flat-screen wonders for "Pillar the Killer," he was too busy to worry about any of that. Physically he is an imposing specimen, a burly torso stuffed into an off-the-rack suit giving the appearance of someone who had done manual labor his whole life and only recently begun adapting to the white-collar world. He projects an aura of dissatisfaction wherever he goes, and whatever this might cost him in his personal life, it has most of our staff thoroughly cowed.

I stood before his desk and again the feeling of having done something wrong, of being in some sort of trouble, elbowed its way to the front of my mind. I ached to speak, to somehow ease the mood, to ask about the weather, the upcoming playoffs, anything, but I didn't want to break whatever train of thought was whizzing through his mind right now. After another agonizing moment, some part of his mind seemed to recognize the presence of another creature, and he gestured vaguely, saying only "Sit."

I sat.

And waited.

And waited some more.

By now my sense of danger had been stoked to roaring levels, and I felt the way a small animal must feel as it crouches within sight of a hungry predator. I thought back to a history course in college, in which we had learned that during interrogations, the Nazi Gestapo had been masters at sustaining tension through silence and vague gestures, until finally their victims would scream confessions without ever being asked anything. I understood how that could be true—at this moment, I was willing to confess to the Lindbergh kidnapping if it would relieve this hellish tension. And still he didn't even look at me!

At length, he said, with his eyes still on his monitor, "Do you know what you're doing here, Joanne?"

I wanted to say, "Dying slowly." But I restrained myself and struggled for a bright, carefree tone as I answered, "No sir, but it's a lucky thing you called. I had been hoping for a chance to ask you a favor."

He grunted, eyes still fixed on his glowing screen. "A favor," he said slowly, as though the word were foreign to him.

All of my animal instincts were screaming, "Run!" but I managed to keep my voice light as I continued. "Yes sir, at this morning's BBS Steering Committee meeting we were discussing how well things are going, and we thought it would be nice to organize a small celebration for the staff to congratulate them, you know, and I said I'd ask you whether you might like to say a few encouraging words to everyone to kick things off."

He said nothing, and still he had not looked at me. Was public speaking not his strong suit? I hurried to reassure him: "Nothing too formal or anything, just your basic pat-on-the-back, keep-up-the-good-work kinda thing, is all…"

I trailed off. He had finally turned his head, ever so slightly, to look my way, and his eyes were as flat and empty as a doll's eyes. What the hell was going on here?

He again repeated my words as if tasting them, deciding whether to make a meal of me. "A pat on the back? For all the good work?"

I nodded. "Yes sir, and of course you wouldn't have to stay, the celebration would con—"

"There's not going to be any celebration."

His words hung strangely in the office. Had I heard him right? "I'm sorry sir, no celebration?"

"There's nothing to celebrate. Your program is a disaster and I've called you up here to find out what you plan to do about fixing it." He stared at me, his distaste apparent as he waited for a response I couldn't even begin to frame.

I fought for composure. "Sir, with all due respect, I don't think our program is anything like a dis—"

He turned back to his monitor, cutting me off with, "Are you aware that as of this morning, you and your program have cost the entire management team our Gold Performance Awards and our annual bonuses?"

I had literally no response for this. I felt as though I was somewhere far away, watching myself like they say you do when you're dying after a car crash. My mouth moved, but no sounds came out. He tapped his screen. "Two hundred thousand dollars in stock options, Joanne. Per man. Gone. They're not happy about it. Neither am I."

I found my voice enough to say, "I don't understand, sir, how could—"

"You don't need to say you don't understand! Your lack of understanding is profoundly obvious and wholly unsupportable!" With this he turned to face me fully for the first time since I had entered. Had I really been hoping for his full attention a moment ago? His full attention was a dreadful thing, a thing to be fled, but I was rooted in place as he continued, his voice growing angrier with every syllable.

"Have you noticed, in the midst of all your plans for your celebration, there's been an increase in accidents of between eleven and seventeen percent, on every shift? Do you mind telling me how it is you think an increase in accidents somehow makes a safety program worthy of a CELEBRATION??"

This last word had been shouted as he rose, slamming his desk with both hands, and I flinched…but some stupid part of me thought logic might actually have a say in this room, and the fact was his question did have a logical answer. I raised my hands, placating, trying to buy time for my answer to make headway.

"Sir, you're describing a reporting issue, it's true the number of reported minor incidents is up, but that's because under our new program reporting itself is up. I believe there are actually fewer injuries but more are actually being reported and that's a good thing, when people trust the process enough to do this kind of reporting then—"

"A good thing," he said, shaking his head as though he were a parent disappointed in a particularly slow-witted child. "My Director of Safety is standing here telling me more accidents is 'a good thing' and I'm supposed to do what, agree with you?"

I was off balance, waiting for the next desk-slamming eruption, but while he was quiet I felt I needed to press my point. "It's diagnostic sir, think about medicine, there's not more cancer now than there was fifty years ago, but our detection and diagnostic techniques are so good that more is being found, more is being reported, it's just information, and it's information we can use, we can—"

"Oooohhhhh, I see, it's only 'information,' well that's a huge relief, I'll just let the Board know that, I'll say something like, "Yes, our overall accident count is higher than last year, but don't let that worry you because our Director of Safety has assured me this is only information.""

"Sir, if you'd—"

"Tell me about Doug Sloan." His flat command caught me by surprise, and his eyebrows lifted a fraction. "You're not going to tell me he's 'only information' too, are you?"

His constant interruptions and shifting focus had me on my heels, but it was also making me angry. "No sir, Mr. Sloan is a valued employee and he was injured reaching into a chute to free up the flow after the machine cycle on Press 32 had been accelerated past the recommended rate."

Pillar rolled his eyes, "This gets better and better, you're telling me our newer and safer plant now includes running machines faster than we're supposed to?"

"No sir," I shot back, "I'm telling you that when you and your management team veto the purchase of new equipment, and fail to provide the appropriate maintenance budget for the old equipment, the plant tends to fall behind schedule, and when you yell about being behind schedule the workers tend to make mistakes attempting to keep you happy, sir."

I knew this had been a mistake the moment the words were out. Dammit Joanne, I thought despairingly, he bullied you into making a mistake.

His eyes narrowed, "You're saying this incident is somehow *my* fault?" he asked with quiet menace.

I shook my head vehemently, backup, try to save something here, "No sir, it's not about blame, I'm trying—look, sir, the issues you raise are just a matter of misunderstanding. I would be more than happy to speak to the Management Team and explain the ways the new program is actually improv—"

He barked a single syllable of what might have been laughter. "No, I don't think that will be necessary, they're already unhappy enough with you. You may recall it was on your recommendation that we set the goal of zero lost-time accidents as the mark for our awards and incentives."

Was this even happening? The entire Management Team blaming me? I shook my head frantically. "No sir, that's not true!"

He pointed an accusing finger at me and bellowed, "You stood in front of my entire staff and told all of us that Zero Lost Time Accidents was an appropriate target!"

"It *is* an appropriate target for safety, but I never told anyone to tie performance bonuses to it!"

Pillar's face was getting red and he was shaking with anger. "You said it! You said it and I backed you up and now it's several incidents and one hundred fifty thousand dollars later and you're telling me it's not what you meant?"

I felt like Alice, down the rabbit hole and into a world where up was down and day was night, nothing made any sense. Money, he's talking about money now, stay with him, Joanne. "A program of this size requires expert implementation, you and the team approved that one hundred fifty thousand so we could retain the largest consulting firm in the business and sir, please, the results are good, if you'll just let me—"

"NO!" He had his hands up in a clear warning that only a fool would have ignored. "No, no, no. I'm done 'just letting you' do anything. If you add that one hundred fifty grand to the lost bonuses, it means letting you do things your way has cost us over a million dollars! No, it's stopping now. Our Quality Program achieved far better results with far less expense; we're going to see what we can salvage here. Do you know Jeff Snyder?"

I was so busy trying to figure out what was happening that it took a moment for my brain to catch up with his question. He eyed me skeptically as I said, "Snyder, no sir, I mean, I know who he is, but I haven't worked with him."

"Well, you're working with him now. He's the one who ran our Quality Program, and he clearly knows some methods you could stand to learn. I want you to get in touch with him and set up a meeting ASAP to talk about how he structured his program and what recommendations he has for you."

"Sir—"

His hand went up to stop me. "Then, you will draft your own plan, based on Jeff's recommendations, for how you will salvage this colossal waste of company time and money. You will have this plan on my desk in two weeks' time, or you'll find yourself exploring career options for former Directors of Safety who squander their employer's resources, are we clear?"

Clear. Nothing was clear except that this meeting was over, a fact he punctuated by sitting down and returning his attention to his monitor as he said, curtly, "We're done here."

Done. My program, my excitement, maybe even my job. Done.

I moved quickly from his office, taking some small pride in the fact that I held back my tears until I was out of Barbara's sight.

CHAPTER 3

"If you don't change directions, you're likely to end up where you're headed."
—Confucius

THE MORNING MEETINGS, my confidence in the rewards the day would bring, the unexpected volcanic eruption in Pillar's office—all have led to here and now. I find myself hiding at my desk, in the middle of some kind of anxiety attack. Short of breath, heart pounding like a trip hammer and my thoughts whirling and unfocused. I rub mindlessly at my forearm and note dimly a tenderness. I glance and see there's a red area that will probably start showing as a bruise in a few hours, a souvenir of my flight from Pillar's office.

As I had hurried toward the elevators, my vision blurred from the tears I was holding back, I turned a corner and slammed right into Donna Andrews carrying two cardboard boxes of files. Donna, the files and I had all gone down in a crash that was more spectacular than damaging. I hurriedly helped her repack the boxes, she'd asked why I was in such a hurry and I'd said, "Just wasn't looking, it was an accident."

Donna, who is on the BBS steering committee with me, had smiled. "You mean 'incident' don't you? Isn't that the term you said we had to use?"

I couldn't worry about vocabulary right then. "Yeah, incident, that's right, sorry," and then we had each gone our own way.

Now I've got a soon-to-be-bruise on my arm to remind me of all the other bruises Pillar has inflicted. The question of "How did this happen?" is no longer so compelling to me. Even in the confused maze of my thoughts, I understand at some basic level there was nothing I could have done to avoid this. Through circumstances entirely beyond my control, I have ended up in the crosshairs of a self-absorbed monster whose plaques and bonuses mean more to him than his workers.

Knowing this doesn't really help much. When you find yourself being chased by a rabid dog, knowing it's not your fault doesn't save you. What the hell am I going to do? Can I protect myself? Is there anyone I can go to for help?

As my mind races through these questions, my eyes pause on the pictures on my desk. Here, my husband Keith, smiling through the sunshine on a camping trip. There, Keith and the kids—Jessica, thirteen, and Matthew, fifteen—all waving from the log flume ride at King's Gardens. Happy, smiling people who love me…but the sunny past from which they're smiling might as well be Mars. There's nothing sunny about today. There's nothing to smile about.

And what will they think of me when I get home? Last night's dinner was filled with confident chatter about my imminent success today. What would tonight's dinner-table conversation be? "Kids, mommy and daddy need to talk to you. We're going to have to cut back on some things, because mommy is about to lose her job. A bad man was mean to her and he's making her leave."

My head shakes reflexively at this track of thought. No. No, no, no, no. I did not reach this position in life just so I could curl up weeping like some little girl when trouble comes. Pillar's an ass. Fine. Deal with it, Joanne.

But how. What to do, how to do it…how do you deal with a crazy person who won't listen to reason and who has absolute power over you…is there any way to deal with that kind of person? Can't fight him, at least not directly… go over his head? No, that won't work, they're an old-boys network, they trust him a helluva lot more than they trust me…Step one is appease him, keep him calm…Jeff.

I'M SUPPOSED TO CALL JEFF. Jeff in Quality, Jeff, Jeff who…Snyder, that was it, Jeff Snyder. What will I say? "Hi, Jeff! We don't know each other but apparently I'm incompetent and you're the big strong man who can teach the poor addled gal how to run her shop!" I feel a spark of anger and take a deep breath to calm myself. Anger beats panic hands down, but it won't do to get mad at this guy. He doesn't even know me, and he certainly has no idea of the position Pillar has just put him in. In a way, we both have something to be mad about, but not at each other.

I find his extension and punch it in. He answers on the first ring, prompt and professional, "This is Jeff Snyder."

I pause half a second. I should have at least considered how to start. Into the pause he speaks again, "Hello?"

Jump in, "Hi Jeff, this is Joanne Cruse from Safety."

"Oh, hey!" His voice brightens, probably with the simple knowledge there really is someone at the other end of the line. "Listen, I understand congrats are in order, people are saying some awfully good things about your program down there."

It's amazing how much this tiny piece of praise does for my nerves. "Thanks, we're all very pleased with it. Or, I guess I should say I thought we were."

"Oh yeah? What changed? It's not that guy hurting his arm, is it? I heard that was no big deal."

I never fail to be struck by the way information can fly around. "No, Mr. Sloan is fine, it's not that. It's—okay let me start over. I had a meeting with Mr.

Pillar a little while ago, and he's not happy with our progress. In fact, that's why I'm calling you."

I hear Jeff exhale. "If you're calling me hoping I know some secret to keeping him happy, then this is gonna be the shortest phone call in history."

My ears perk up. I had assumed Jeff was some kind of staunch Pillar disciple, but maybe not. Maybe even an ally? "Is that right?" I ask, striving for a casual tone.

"Well…" He's suddenly hesitant, and I don't blame him. He's caught himself teetering on the edge of badmouthing the boss to someone he doesn't even know. He speaks more slowly now, "All I can tell you is my experiences with him when I was implementing our new QC program made it clear he's a very hard man to please. But hey, what boss isn't, right?" A strained, politically-correct chuckle.

Two weeks or else. Go for broke. "Listen Jeff, I'm under some pressure here, so I'm going to be very frank with you, and if it gets me in hot water, then so be it, I'm already in boiling water up to my eyeballs. I just came from a meeting with him—Pillar I mean—and he tore my head clean off, and I'm still not exactly sure what I'm supposed to do. But he specifically ordered me to call you because you'd had so much success with your program."

He laughs incredulously. "He said that?"

"He did indeed. He seemed very impressed with you."

Jeff snorts, "Well, its news to me. The whole time I was putting that thing into motion, he picked at every decision. When it was done and obviously working well—on time and under budget, by the way—you know what he said to me? He looked at my report and said, 'Okay, that's done.' So, you know—you can see why I'm surprised to hear he said anything so complimentary."

Jeff is my new best friend. "Well, he did. And apparently you're supposed to save me from my own shortcomings."

I can hear him smiling. "You're taking it a lot better than I would have. I never met anyone who can find so many things wrong with something that's working fine. Unless it's a budget he created, and then there's nothing wrong with it no matter how much is wrong with it, you know what I mean? Anyway. What exactly is it he thinks I can do for you?"

The question brings me up short. It's the right question, and I have no idea how to answer it. The bright spot which this conversation has been suddenly fades. "I'm not sure. All I know is he said my program is a shambles, you had shown how to run an effective program for less money, and I should get with you so you can help me fix things."

He sighs, "That's brilliant. And then afterwards maybe he'd like me to go down and fix some of the machinery on the floor, I mean, I don't know anything about safety, and I sure wouldn't think to advise you about any of it."

We're taking a wrong turn—I need help, not a list of why it won't work. "Maybe just a fresh set of eyes to look at things, Jeff, all I know is, he gave me two weeks to get things fixed."

"Two weeks, huh? Kind of arbitrary. Or else what?"

The bluntness of this brings all the anxiety back, front and center. Keep my voice calm. "Or else I'm out."

Jeff makes a disgusted sound. "What an ass. Okay, look, Joanne, I don't know what I can do, but I'm happy to look things over, maybe like you say, maybe new eyes will see something. I'm pretty slammed for the rest of the day, you wanna have some lunch tomorrow?"

I'm nodding to myself, "Sure, lunch tomorrow would be perfect. Meet in the lobby?"

"Yeah, good, twelve-thirty okay for you?"

"Absolutely. Thank you, Jeff."

He laughs, "Let's wait until after the meeting to see whether you have anything to thank me for. See ya tomorrow."

We hang up and the sense of desolation comes rushing back in. Okay, sure, it's nice to know I'm not the only one who finds Pillar difficult, but so what? It's like Jeff said, what on earth can he do to help? Our BBS program is detailed and intricate, designed by the best consultants money can buy and it's the result of their years of experience. Moreover, it's working! There's nothing to fix! What on earth is some QC guy gonna do to make any kind of difference? What do I do?

What do I do? The thought loops in my head like a kind of chant: What do I do? What do I do? What…

A knock at the door. "Joanne?"

I recognize the voice. Armelia. She's one of the administrative assistants on the floor. I don't rate my own secretary, but there are a couple of people who float to help keep the paperwork at bay. "Yeah, Armelia, come on in."

Armelia sticks her head in. She looks a little hesitant. "You need anything?"

I shake my head, confused. "No, why?"

She shrugs, "I thought I heard you banging on something in here."

That's when I notice the numbness in the fingertips of my right hand, and I realize the absent-minded tapping I had done to accompany my "what do I do" refrain must have gotten pretty forceful. I summon a smile and say, "No, I, um, had this song stuck in my head."

Armelia smiles, "Gonna be a drummer, huh?"

In two weeks maybe so. I keep the fake smile plastered on, "Ya never know."

She nods, "Okay, well if you need me, just…drum some more." She closes the door gently behind her.

I take another deep breath. I'm officially losing all usefulness. I can't think straight, I'm making noises I'm not even aware of, I gotta get out of here. Take the rest of the day as personal time.

I won't be missed. After all, according to the boss I'm not achieving anything anyway.

DRIVING HOME IN MY CAR, I'm distantly aware of the strangeness of things. Early afternoon on the freeway is so different from rush hour, and I have that feeling you used to get when you left school early for a doctor's appointment or something, and you got a glimpse of what the world is doing at times that are normally hidden. The light is different. Shadows are different. Everything's different…

…but those observations are all surface. Deep down, I'm stuck in that fearful loop of confusion. What do I do? What do I do? He's crazy. No, he's not crazy, he's greedy. So what do you do? Greedy people can be bought, right? Yeah, but not with anything I have. What do I do? What do I do?

In the distance, I register a car on the shoulder and someone at its rear, bending to examine something. Probably a flat. Welcome to the world, folks. This is what happens—you're driving along, everything is great, and suddenly, out of nowhere, *boom*, you're knocked off the road. Get used to it.

As I drive by, my bitterness is replaced by a kind of delayed surprise—is that my neighbor's kid Katie? It looks like her VW Beetle, and I catch a glimpse of a forlorn face that sure looks like her...but before I can be sure, the scene is receding rapidly in my rearview mirror and I hear the loud *whirrrrrrr* which tells me I've eased onto the shoulder. I correct quickly, returning my eyes to the road in front of me.

To hell with it. Every kid nowadays has a cell phone, it's practically a law. If it was Katie, she's called for help by now. It's not like I'm any whiz at changing tires anyway.

Still, I think about it again as I pull into my neighborhood. I glance toward her driveway, maybe it was some other VW and hers will be home...nope, not there. Probably was her. What's she gonna tell her folks? "I thought I saw Miz Cruse but she just drove right past." Perfect. Like it's my job to play Good Samaritan on the roadways, like I'm not already having a complicated enough day...

The sense of differentness which flickered through my mind on the freeway is amplified as I move down our street. Young mothers with strollers. Panel trucks, there's one installing carpeting (we were gonna do that, I think to myself, back when I still had a job) and there's one fixing someone's heat pump (wonder if they fix bosses), but most of the driveways are empty of their usual mid-size imports...until I catch sight of our driveway and see Keith's Camry.

I thought I was out of adrenaline, but here we go again, heart pounding and that metallic taste in my mouth. Why is Keith home? What's wrong? Is it one of the kids? Or is it more surreal, am I about to walk in on Keith and one of the divorcees from down the street? Don't be stupid, Joanne! Fine, I won't, but what's he doing home at this hour?

My car lurches to a stop in the driveway and I'm out in a flash, moving in a walk that's trying not to be a run. I'm through the front door and calling in a loud voice, "Keith?!

He appears at the kitchen door, his blond, surfer-boy good looks frozen in a state of surprise, "What are you doing home?"

Not the most reassuring of opening lines. I drop my purse on the table by the door. "I was about to ask you the same thing, is something wrong, are the kids okay?"

He seems strangely nonplussed. "Who? The, oh, okay, yes, they're fine, I mean, I guess they are, I haven't, um, heard, you know, anything from them."

My head shakes a fraction as I try to filter this utter lack of useful information. I step towards him. "Well, what're you doing home so early?"

He actually takes a tiny step backward. Away from me? Am I poison to everyone today? "I'm, you know, I needed to get some, hey don't come in here!"

He has actually spread his arms to block my entering the kitchen. What the hell is going on? I can feel the anger in me prowling, looking for some excuse to unload, and my voice comes out clipped and measured. "I'm hungry. In fact, I'm starving."

He's still blocking me from my own kitchen, actually side-stepping to stay in front of me. "What, you missed lunch, is that why you came home?"

Usually I like being married to a guy who's six-two and weighs two-twenty but right now it's getting on my nerves. I've been stymied by men enough today. I can't stand another second of this. "Yes, I missed lunch. No, that is not why I came home. Now would you please get out of my way!"

But he doesn't. He lifts his hands as though to keep me at bay and says, "Let me do it, what would you like?"

I snap, "What I'd like is for you to get the hell out of my way so I can get something to eat in my own damned house and then maybe you'd do me the favor of letting me know what you're doing here in the middle of the day!"

Incredibly, he shakes his head and plants himself, "Can't do it."

He's got that smile I always think of as his frat-boy smile, it means he's up to something, and at this moment it is the last thing I want to see on his face. The entire morning comes pouring out of my mouth: "Would you get out of my way and let me get a sah-sah-sah-AHHhhhhhhh!" and before I know it I'm sobbing, great, shuddering things that wrack me from head to toe, and then his arms are around me, whether holding me or restraining me I can't tell.

"Hey, hey, what, what is this, sshhhhhh, okay…okay…ssshhhhh… " I can hear the alarm in his voice, and at least that's something, at least he finally understands there are bigger forces at work here, and whatever he thought was happening is going to have to be set aside.

I don't know how long we stand like this, but eventually my sobs give way to shuddering breaths and I realize I feel slightly better. Keith. Home. Yes this is better. I pull away from him just enough to look up at him. "I'm suh-suh-sorry, I've huh-had a really buh-buh-bad day…"

He continues to hold me, stroking my hair with his large hands. "Shhh, okay…it's okay."

I shake my head into his chest. "No. It's not okay, it's a long way from okay."

He looks down. "Tell me?"

I pull slowly away from him, turning aside so I can step back and breathe. He deserves to hear everything, of course he does, but somehow I can't start. "Could I please get something to eat first?"

He steers me toward my favorite chair. "Yes, you may, and what's more, I will get it and bring it to you like the good houseboy you've trained me to be—how about some turkey on rye, a little Dijon mustard, a little cheddar, how's that?"

I manage a smile up to him, grateful to be relieved of any decisions. "Heaven."

"Coming up!" and just like that he's back into the kitchen.

With the wisdom that can only come from twenty-two years of marriage, he doesn't ask any questions while he works, and I'm not ready to tell the story yet. After a few moments of silence I remember the drive home and I say, "Hey, you know what? I think I saw Katie McCauley on my way home."

"Oh yeah?" he answers in his I'm-listening-but-I'm-busy voice.

"Yeah," I continue, "I passed her on the freeway, she was on the side of the road, I think she had a flat."

A knife on a chopping board, and "That would suck."

"I felt bad about going right past her, but you know, I was moving so fast, by the time I was past her it was too late to do anything."

"Don't you have her number in your cell from her old baby-sitting days?"

"I dunno, maybe, why?"

"Well, you could have called. See if she's okay. See if it was really her, too."

Men are so thick. Why can't a man ever listen to a problem and be sympathetic, why must they always suggest things? Even after my meltdown, he's right back into fix-it mode. Doesn't he know all I need right now is for him to say, "Don't worry babe, I'm sure she phoned her folks and she's already fixed up and on her way." Instead he tells me what I should have done.

Maybe some part of me wants to avoid the real issue, but the next thing I know I'm snapping at him again: "I didn't have the time to think about it, I was already kind of in the middle of my own problems which—trust me—are a lot worse than a few minutes with a flat tire, you know?"

"Okay, okay." He has emerged with a restaurant-perfect sandwich and a conciliatory look. "You're right, sorry."

I take the plate and immediately take an enormous bite. "Mmm, fanks…" I manage through my full mouth.

"Was that 'thanks'?" he asks. I nod, chewing. He gives a little bow. "Well, you're welcome."

I nod again. He's trying to be cute, to be light-hearted, to cheer me up, and it's not that I don't appreciate it, and the sandwich…but you know how sometimes you just don't want to feel better, at least not until everyone really understands just how bad things are? I found myself resenting his upbeat attitude. I try to keep a lid on it. "So you never told me what you're doing home."

"Oh yeah…" He appears to be weighing something, and to his credit, he decides to set aside whatever ideas he'd had about things. "Well, it was gonna be a secret. I wanted to throw you a little celebratory dinner. I even got out the good stuff." He gestures toward the dining room, and I notice for the first time the elegant place settings, complete with our best crystal and china. He continues, "You've been working so hard, and you were so excited about your meeting today, and I thought …you know."

He trails off, and now I feel like an even bigger failure than ever. My boss says I've ruined his life, and now my husband is making it clear I've ruined his dinner party. What a perfect day. I chew in silence, the food suddenly like cardboard in my mouth.

He tries again, "So anyway, I guess your day wasn't as good as you hoped, but maybe a nice dinner will cheer you up? The kids will get a kick out of eating so fancy."

Great. Bring our kids into it, that way I'll feel really good. I'm feeling more mulish by the second, even though some distant part of me knows I'm behaving like a child. "You know what, Keith? I'm not sure I'm gonna be up to any kind of special thing tonight."

He stiffens a bit, and I can feel him striving for the correct tone through his disappointment. "Well…okay. Maybe you'll change your mind after you've calmed down a little bit."

"I'm calm."

"You're calmer," he says evenly, and whether he knows it or not he's moving into instructive mode again, and if he can't feel the ice crackling under his feet then he's about to get very wet. "But I wouldn't say you're calm. Do you think you could manage to tell me what happened?"

Oh, please, don't you see, don't you know the answer to that, I'm not sure I can without crying and I'll be damned if I'll cry again, I'm not gonna let anybody bully me into something that would make me cry again, how dare you seem so inconvenienced by this, you know what, you want it, fine, get ready: "Yes, Keith, I imagine I could manage to tell you, I'm assuming you mean without any further hysterical outbursts, is that right?"

He looks at me for a long moment, and then moves to rise. "You're upset. I shouldn't push, okay, I get it. You take all the time you…" he stops suddenly and his eyes narrow as he sees the mark on my arm. "What happened there?"

"Where?"

"Right there, that mark on your arm, what'd you do?"

Again something inside of me simply lets go, like a wire under too much stress. "What'd I do, yes, of course, it must have been something I did, well you're right, what I did was I came around a corner without looking and I knocked

Donna and her papers ass-over-teakettle and one of her boxes clipped me, and what was I doing walking so fast is what you're wondering so here, I was walking as fast as I could to get away from a meeting with Bob Pillar in which he more or less fired me, okay?"

Keith is very still now. "Fired."

I throw my hands into the air. "Not technically, but give it two weeks and it's the same thing, so there, that's the news, Safety Jo's out, okay?"

I can see him getting angry, and some animal part of me actually leans into this, yes, good, let's fight, let's do it, anything to keep the real problem at bay… and then I realize that in spite of how horrible I'm being, he's not angry with me. He's angry with Pillar. His voice is very quiet, and I learned a long time ago the only time Keith is quiet is when someone is in very, very big trouble. "Bob Pillar gave you notice. After all you've done for that company? You're fired?"

Without a moment's warning, everything inside me does a one-eighty. He's on my side. He's furious that someone did this to me. A big part of him wants to go see Pillar right now—the middle-linebacker Keith would like to go wait for Pillar in the parking lot, and I cannot tell you how good it makes me feel to know this man will always be right here ready to go to war for me. It never fails to amaze me: Our problems always feel so complicated, but the things that make us feel good are always so simple. A good sandwich. Belongingness. Love.

So I tell him the whole story, from the first meeting until this very moment, when I've seen the flare of rage in my husband's eyes which would just as soon tear Pillar limb from limb. "But I'm not sure he can be killed, except maybe with a stake through the heart," I finish.

Keith laughs, and that's good, and I laugh with him, and that's better. We talk some more, with Keith's clear agenda being to make sure I feel okay. We talk around the edges of the big "what if" of my future employment, and again Keith does everything he can to make me feel safe. "We've got savings, I've got two huge commissions coming in, and there's no way they could let you go without some kind of decent

severance package. You're highly employable, you'd land on your feet. Maybe even enjoy a couple months off before you go back to the rat race."

I shake my head vehemently, "I don't want a couple months off. I've worked for almost fifteen years making sure we're all safer every year than we were the year before. At one level, it's not even about me and my paycheck, it's about them, you know? About making a difference for every one of us who works here. I don't want to give that up."

He shrugs, "Then don't."

I start slightly, "What?"

"Don't," he repeats. "Don't give it up. You're smart, you're tough, and you've got time to figure this thing out. You've got a meeting tomorrow with a guy who doesn't like Pillar any more than you do, who knows what ideas you guys might have?"

"Yeah, but—"

"No buts," he pronounces firmly. "You're exhausted, and you don't need to keep throwing yourself against this problem tonight, it'll still be there tomorrow."

"How comforting," I answer dryly.

"Ain't I though?" he grins. "So, here's what's gonna happen: You're gonna let me get back to my chicken, which I promise you is gonna make you think you died and went to heaven. You're gonna go upstairs and have a nice long soak in that damned antique tub you couldn't live without, and then we're going to have an absolutely perfect family dinner."

"You say that with such confidence, sir."

He tips an invisible cowboy hat. "Just doin' m' job, ma'am. Now git on upstairs."

Keith's predictions are pretty much dead on. I have a luxurious long bath, feeling like some kind of royalty as I soak with Josh Groban in the background, imagining all the other poor slobs in the world fighting rush hour. After my bath, Keith has a perfectly chilled glass of white wine ready for me, and then before I know it we're all at the table, listening to my son Matthew tell some goofy story about his friend trying to Photo-Shop Jimmy Fallon's head onto his PE teacher for the yearbook, and then Jessica weighs in asking our opinions about whether she should try to answer an anonymous love letter she found in her locker (rejecting every single suggestion, naturally) and all in all, life is pretty good.

We talk only in a brief and cursory way about my problems, which the table immediately christens as "Mom's jerk-face boss" and we laugh about all the different ways we could get even…but what really matters is that we're together, not just around the table, but in spirit. I lean back for a moment to watch the three of them laughing, and feel a surge of gratitude. I'm a lucky woman.

LATER, AS I'M GETTING READY for bed, I catch sight of my new bruise in the mirror. It strikes me as deeply symbolic somehow. I have emerged from my battle with Pillar—bruised, but still standing.

Of course, it didn't really happen until after the meeting, and I have a moment to wonder whether Donna is finding any new marks on herself tonight. Then I wonder whether she thought to fill out any kind of report on the incident. My insides clench up again for a moment—if she did file a report, and I didn't, then that would look pretty bad, more fuel for Pillar's hellfire… but I doubt she did. She didn't seem to care about anything but getting her papers in order, thank goodness.

Then even that thought strikes a dissonant chord. Here stands the Safety Director, feeling grateful an injury is going unreported so she won't be in trouble. This is exactly the mindset I've spent years trying to defeat. Pillar's got me jumping at shadows and behaving in ways antithetical to my safety mission for the company.

I hadn't even used the right language when it happened. I needed one of our committee members to correct me. "Accident." Hardly anything's an "accident." If it could have been prevented and wasn't, then it's an incident. How many times have I pounded this exact point in meetings?

I shake my head at the mirror, and my reflection shakes her head back at me. No more. Tomorrow I go back to being Joanne Cruse, Safety Goddess. Keith is right—maybe my meeting with Jeff will give me some fresh insight about how to handle this mess. Time to sleep on it.

Keith is already snoring lightly, and I feel a powerful surge of affection for him. I don't know anyone who could have had the day I've had and then come home to this much support, this much comfort. I kiss his sleeping face lightly and then settle gratefully into bed, wriggling under the comforter and ready to let slumber take hold.

But as I lie awake, all of my temporary comforts feel like a small pool of light, with looming darkness all around…and in that darkness, a clock, ticking, counting down the minutes I have to find some way to save myself. I check to see that my alarm is set. Past midnight already.

Thirteen days left.

It's a long time before I manage to sleep.

CHAPTER 4

"If you want to get a good idea, get a lot of ideas."
— Linus Pauling

LUNCHTIME THE NEXT DAY finds me a passenger in Jeff's BMW, wondering how such a young man can afford such a nice car. He can't be much over thirty, but I guess being the company's QC Superstar carries some compensation…and the fact he's single leaves him with a little more money for toys.

He had said he was in the mood for Mexican, which was fine, but then he'd suggested a popular restaurant close to the plant, and I had felt a twinge of discomfort at the thought of co-workers seeing us together. I didn't feel like navigating any questions or quizzical glances that might come our way, and so

I'd countered with a place further down the highway. He'd shrugged and said it was okay with him.

Riding along now and making small talk, a part of me is diverted by this unexpected desire to avoid our colleagues. It wasn't as if Jeff and I had anything to hide, but I didn't feel like explaining the truth of the situation to anyone either: "Oh yes, well, you see, the GM feels I'm incompetent, so he's asked me to get some pointers from the local wunderkind who has no background in safety but who does drive a hot car." Too complicated, too awkward. If that makes me a coward, so be it.

As we move down the freeway, I notice that Jeff hasn't fastened his safety belt. I almost mention it and then bite my tongue. I'm already keenly aware of the difference in our ages and I'll be damned if I'm going to play mommy and nag him about being safe. Still, it's an alien feeling—I seem to be finding ways to avoid moments which I would normally skim through without a moment's pause. I'm definitely off my game. Pillar again.

The topper is my sight of the same VW bug I had driven by yesterday, now abandoned on the roadside with a pitiful white handkerchief wedged in the driver's side window. Jeff notices my dismay and asks if I know the car, and I give him the short version, simply mentioning I think it belongs to a neighbor kid. I don't tell him about the sinking feeling in my stomach, as I wonder whether she's okay and if my failure to stop and help yesterday might have really cost her something. There it is again—I avoided something which normally would have been natural to me, and now I'm fighting waves of guilt as I imagine the various things that might have happened to her.

Jeff dismisses it with an airy wave of his hand. "Trust me," he says, "She had Daddy on her cell phone within seconds, calling in the cavalry. She's probably at the dealership right now picking out her new one. 'I can't drive the old one, it's busted!'" We laugh at his pitch-perfect replica of the new generation's embrace of all things disposable.

MOMENTS LATER WE'RE TURNING into the parking lot of Casa Grande ("I wonder if they know they named their restaurant 'The Prison,' " Jeff jokes), and then we're being shown to a table in the rear where everything is cool shadows and the tangy smell of chiles.

Once we've settled in and both ruefully declined the basketball-sized margaritas and ordered our lunches (a gigantic combo platter for him, and chicken chimichangas for me), it becomes clear we've used up whatever small talk we had available, and there's nothing left but to address my problem head on.

"I really appreciate you taking this time to help me out, Jeff. I'm pretty much stuck. I have no idea what Pillar expects me to do, and I—"

"He expects you to take the fall for his buddies not getting their bonuses."

His gaze is direct and without humor, and I can only stare back, startled that such an abrupt assessment could come so quickly from someone I just met. I speak slowly. "Well, yeah, that might be one way to look at it, but my problem is—"

"It's not one way to look at it, it's the way things are. Look, Joanne, I need to tell you something that's bugging me and I wanted to wait until we were face-to-face to do it."

A fresh stab of fear, something I'm getting both strangely used to and terribly tired of. "Okay," I say, "what is it?"

Jeff takes a deep breath, gathering himself and then says, "Pillar called me this morning wondering if you had gotten in touch with me yet. I told him you had and we were meeting for lunch."

I relax a bit. "Well, that's not a surprise, he's just checking up on me, maybe he's hoping I forgot so he can hammer me with being disobedient along with everything else."

Jeff shakes his head ruefully. "He wants to hammer you, but it's deeper than that. He told me he wants me to call him back after our lunch so I can keep him posted. He said he wants specific reports about your plans, and I got the very distinct impression he doesn't expect you to come up with much. He didn't say it in so many words, but I think he was giving me a green light to give him bad reports about you. He's making me his mole in your operation. And it makes me sick to my stomach."

It feels as though the floor is tipping a bit, and I struggle for some way to keep things level. I try for an even tone. "Okay, well, I already knew he didn't think much of what I was doing, and the fact that he only gave me two weeks meant he was probably looking to scapegoat me, but still, that doesn't mean he's recruiting you for sabotage. After all, he told me to call you, maybe it's really as simple as monitoring our progress."

Jeff snorts. "You're saying maybe he was just doing his job, just managing."

I nod. "Exactly."

"Yeah, well if that were true, he'd be asking me how I plan to help. He'd be pushing me to do what I can to help save the program, he'd be trying to achieve something positive, right? But all he's looking to do is to get a third-party confirmation of his own bad opinion of you. He's not looking to fix anything, he's looking to solidify his case for letting you go."

Suddenly I'm wishing I had ordered that margarita. I lean back in my chair, as if a little distance from Jeff's words will somehow help me. I start to say something and then stop, realizing there's nothing to say.

But Jeff leans in, and there's an intensity to his voice, "I hate this. And I hate that he thinks he can use me as some kind of cat's paw to hurt someone who, as far as I can tell, has done nothing but good things for the company. I want to get back from this lunch and tell him I'm very surprised and pleased to report that you and I found some excellent ideas for turning things around. So we need to do that, you follow me?"

I consider him from across the table. He's serious. He's mad at Pillar, and he wants to beat him. He's volunteering to be a soldier for my cause. I don't know what good it'll do, but it sure does feel good. "Okay," I say. "So where do we start?"

He spreads his arms. "You tell me. I don't know anything about your program, why don't you start with that, catch me up on what you've been doing and how it's been going."

So as our food arrives I fill him in on the basics of our BBS process. I tell him about how we selected our consulting firm, the biggest and best-known in the world ("and the most expensive?" he'd asked, and my laughter had been my agreement). I give him the groundwork on how BBS works and how it attempts to put safety more in the hands of the workers by focusing on their behavior.

"It's not the same common-sense stuff repackaged into a new set of bullet-points. It's really a whole new way of thinking about how you and your co-workers do things." He nods as he works his way through his food. He clearly gets it, and is processing what I'm saying, and it feels good to be on this familiar turf.

Then I mention the increase in reported small incidents, and why this is a good thing. "The willingness to report and analyze close calls and minor injuries is terribly important, because the only chance we have to learn from our mistakes is to admit them, even the small ones. Sometimes especially the small ones. BBS only works if everyone is painfully, meticulously honest."

"And that's part of Pillar's problem?" Jeff asks. "He's like some doctor from the 1940s saying, 'You have so much more cancer than we ever did!' because he doesn't understand that our detection methods are better?"

I clap my hands. "I used that exact analogy, yes!"

Jeff shakes his head, still forking food into his mouth. "Moron," he mutters. "Okay what else?"

"Well, the last straw seems to be the injury Mr. Sloan suffered last week."

Jeff's eyes narrow, "I thought you said yesterday it wasn't a big deal; that he was going to be fine."

I consider my answer for a moment, "Well, he is going to be fine. But I'm not sure I'd say it's not a big deal—it's a loss-time incident, an employee was injured, it could have been much worse, but we learned a few things from it and I like to think of it as an opportunity. So it is a big deal, but it's nothing of permanent harm. At least that's what I thought."

"Pillar thinks differently," Jeff says as if it's a foregone conclusion, and I had to agree.

"The big problem is when we began the program, Pillar asked if zero injuries was an appropriate goal. Of course I said it was—what kind of Safety Director would I be if I didn't have zero injuries as our target? But then the senior management team inserted zero lost-time incidents as one of the milestones for their annual bonuses. Apparently my desire to strive for perfection has left all of them a quarter million dollars poorer than they expected to be."

Jeff leans back and smiles, "Ahhhhhhh, okay. This is starting to make sense. A horribly twisted stupid sense, for sure, but now I see what the big deal is. It's not about Sloan's arm, it's about their own wallets."

I nod, "I couldn't have said it better myself."

There is a silence in which Jeff seems to be pondering his new understanding of the battlefield, and I take the opportunity to get a bite of the food that's been getting cold while I've filled him in. At length, he speaks musingly, "You know the whole safety field is so stacked."

"Whaddaya mean?" I manage around my mouthful of chicken.

"Well, it's about flesh and blood, you know? We make a mistake in quality, maybe it's big, maybe it's little, but either way no one goes to the hospital, you know?" I nod and he continues, "You know about Six Sigma, right? Well, the Six Sigma mark for my field is three to four defects per million, which puts the bar awfully high, you know?

But I guess if I wanted to translate that to safety, you'd have to think about okay, you've got what, fifty workers on the floor, and for easy math let's say they each make ten decisions a minute, even if most of them are auto-pilot kinds of things, right? So that's five hundred decisions every minute, thirty thousand every hour, so that's what, almost a quarter million every shift, so it only takes four shifts for you to hit a million decisions, and you're having way fewer than three accidents every four shifts. So that means you're making Six Sigma quality levels look like child's play and Pillar is still gonna try to roast you. I call that playing with a stacked deck."

I hold up a finger to slow him down. "You could look at it that way, for sure, but you have to remember the stakes are higher. We have to set our bar higher, because like you say, it's flesh and blood, not a customer needing a replacement part."

Jeff is nodding quickly, "Right, of course, I get that, but what I'm saying is if you're going to be held to that kind of standard, you need the whole company behind you. You need safety to be a big part of everyone's vision of how the company runs. It can't be some compartmentalized thing off in the corner, you know?"

He's making sense but at the same time not making sense. I give him a grin, "I understand all of those words and what they mean, but I'm not sure I get where you're going."

He pushes his plate to the side, clearing the field for his thoughts, "Okay, look. I'm just a quality guy and I might be a million miles off the mark, okay?"

I nod, "Fair enough."

He continues, "But listening to you talking about BBS just now, I started to get the feeling those guys are missing the point."

I start to protest, to remind him that internationally acclaimed specialists in the field had helped us design our program, but he waves me off. "Wait a second, wait a second, hear me out, okay? Their whole thing is that wrong behavior leads to unsafe situations and maybe even accidents, right?"

"Well, basically," I agree. "Our consultants break the behavior into four different areas—complacency, weariness, haste, or inattention, but yeah, they're all different kinds of behavior and the behavior can lead to injuries."

"And I say they're missing the point. They're saying behavior is the cause of the injuries, that behavior is the source and injuries are the outcome; but I'm saying behavior is an outcome too, that they're looking at the middle as though it's the beginning."

There's something in what he's saying that intrigues me. "Keep going," I urge.

"Well look, it's like dominoes, isn't it? You know how you line up dominoes and then knock the first one over and they all go? Well behavior isn't the first domino, it's just the one your consulting firm decided to look at. But what I wanna know is, what causes the behavior? What's the domino that got pushed into that one?"

He leans in, "You know, we used to blame our workers for quality failures. If something leaves a worker's hands and it's not right, it must be the worker's fault, right? Sounds simple. But when we started to look closer we saw that just like a lotta things in life, what looked simple was actually pretty complicated."

Something in me rebels at what I think is coming. "We don't know each other very well Jeff, but I sure hope you're not about to try and sell me some feel-good PC notion about how we're all human and there's no such thing as failure, only opportunity for growth, cause I gotta tell you, in the safety world that stuff doesn't cut it. Unsafe behavior leads to risk, risk leads to injuries, the end. I know it's fashionable nowadays to not hold people accountable for their mistakes, but hey—admitting you screwed up is the first step toward fixing the problem."

Jeff eyes me, "Like you screwed up with Pillar, you're saying."

This brings me up short, "What are you talking about?"

"Well, Pillar is the boss, right? And he says there's a problem and so that means there is a problem, that's what being the boss is all about. So since there's a problem and it came from your desk, you must have screwed up, if I'm hearing you right."

I'm in no mood for trappy word-games. "That doesn't have anything to do with what we're talking about, we're talking about simple accountability and you're trying to—"

"It is what we're talking about, it's exactly what we're talking about." He's leaning closer, and his face and his tone are both no-nonsense. "What we're talking about is the fact that accountability isn't simple, and when people try to make it overly simple they create an unjust environment in which real progress isn't possible." He leans back a bit, relaxing. "Here, look, I'm not trying to accuse you of anything, I'm trying to make a point. Of course you're not accountable for Pillar holding you to some ridiculous standard that he doesn't even bother to define, we both know that. Lemme tell you a story, okay?"

My guard is still up, but I'm curious. "Okay…"

He leans close again, "About fourteen months ago, we had about eight customer complaints that were all more or less the same. Some of our filter lenses were being reported as scratched when they reached the customer. Not big scratches, mind you, they were all in the two micron range, but two microns was more than enough to make them substandard, and so the customers were rightly upset."

He takes a sip of water and continues, "Now, the first complaint, we just passed along with a warning, you know, 'Make sure you're being diligent in following the inspection protocols before you ship the product,' etcetera. Second complaint, we basically did the same thing but in harsher language.

Then we had like four or five complaints come in within a twenty-four-hour period, and it was like 'okay, someone needs to find a new line of work' and we fired the person doing the inspections for that shift and we fired his supervisor. Two days later another complaint comes in but we're feeling okay because that product had been shipped before we fixed things with our magic axe, right? I mean, that many errors, again and again, that's an employee shortcoming pure and simple, accountability and all that, right?"

I can feel myself being painted into some kind of rhetorical corner, but my curiosity is piqued. "Sure, I'd agree with that."

He leans in again, "About four days later, we get word from the union rep of the workers we terminated that they plan to bring grievance charges and they're requesting a hearing. Which is nothing unusual, right, that's what unions do, make it time consuming to fire anyone, but I stick to my guns and say fine, bring it on, let's have a hearing. Later that same day, we get yet another complaint, about a shipment which was inspected after we let those two guys go."

"The plot thickens."

"Yeah, and it's a lot thicker than two microns." He smiles, and continues, "So now I'm like furious, and I go down to the floor myself, you know, all huffy and outraged and 'By Golly, you want something done right you gotta do it yourself, grrr, grrrr' you know? And I demand to see their inspection protocols. I still remember it word for word: 'Holding the product at a distance of eighteen inches, the inspector shall survey the product for no less than ten seconds per item.' And as I read this, I can feel all these people looking at me. We had fired two of their colleagues, you know."

I must be missing something, "I'm sorry, I don't get it."

He smiles, "You know what a micron is, Joanne?"

Ahhhhh, I'm beginning to get where this might be going. "Not really. I mean, I know it's small…"

He laughs, "The thinnest human hair is forty microns thick. There are about twenty-five thousand microns in an inch."

That can't be right, I think. "But—how are they supposed to have seen that just looking at something from a foot and a half away?"

He does a little martial arts-style bow. "You have come far, Grasshopper."

"So what, you're saying…what are you saying?"

He leans in again, suddenly intense, "I'm saying we fired people who were diligently following a protocol which had no chance on this earth of giving us the outcome we needed. I'm saying we fired people for following orders because the orders were crazy and we never even bothered to look into it until after we had a bunch of complaints and a union legal action hanging over our heads. I'm saying their behavior, as inspectors, was an outcome of a flawed process in which they had no voice." He settles back, "I'm saying accountability is a tricky horse to ride."

"What happened with the union?"

He laughs, "We got off pretty cheap. We had to reinstate the workers with all back pay, we had to publish a company-wide apology for our error, and we had to make a small contribution to a charity of the union's choice."

I nod, "That's pretty cheap all right."

"And the best part was, we found the real problem. It wasn't behavior-based. It was procedural, and it was cultural, and it had its genesis way upstream of the so-called worker errors. And so, with all due respect to your consultants, I'm sitting here thinking they may be showing up late to the safety party."

As I try to wrap my mind around this concept, our waiter approaches and asks if we'd like dessert. I've barely eaten half of my lunch and my appetite seems to be missing in action, but Jeff orders some fried ice cream. The boy is a bottomless pit.

As the waiter leaves to fetch the dessert, I speak slowly, thinking out loud, "All right, I can see where bad inspection protocols could generate a behavior for which those particular employees shouldn't be blamed. And we had something like that a couple of years ago. We had an injury which we traced to an unswept floor and we went crazy because proper housekeeping had always been one of our focuses…but when we looked at it closely we found out—you're gonna love this—we found out we had a grand total of two push brooms for a production floor the size of a football field, and all hundred and twenty employees were supposed to sweep their own area every two hours. And I think one of those brooms was actually missing."

He points at his nose, "Bingo. The 'bad' behavior of the faulty housekeeping was an outcome, not a cause."

"Okay," I counter, "but what about Sloan's injury? There was no flawed procedure there, the man reached up inside a machine that was still powered up and he got hurt. We spend hours and hours every year going over stuff like this, you need to lock out the power on any equipment you're working on, don't reach inside any machine that's running, don't grab a chain saw by the blade, you know, common sense stuff, how is he exempt from responsibility here?"

Jeff's eyes are up, as though scanning the ceiling for an answer. "I don't know …but I can tell you people do what they think is in their own best interests. People know not to grab a chain saw by the blade, but this was one guy who thought it was in his best interest to reach up into the machine. I don't know anything about what he was doing, you tell me, how did he imagine he was helping himself?"

It's an interesting question, "Well, I know that even though it's an unsafe behavior, it's not unprecedented. We've reduced the maintenance staff that would normally put in a permanent fix on something like this. And, if he has to power down the machine, the whole line has to pause, and then you've got eight or nine people standing around waiting, and everyone knows we're behind schedule, so…"

He slaps the table lightly. "There it is. What you just said. 'Everyone knows we're behind schedule.' That means it's been a point of conversation, right? Maybe management is leaning on them to step it up?"

It's almost as if he was at yesterday's shift-change meeting. I nod reluctantly, "And it's been discussed as something that needs to be changed, because the workers know it's not fair to lean on them when the equipment keeps breaking down."

He's nodding, "There it is again. Culture. On the one hand we're telling them to be safe, but on the other hand we're telling them we need them to be unsafe. It's a mixed message, and the reckless behavior is an outcome of that mixed message. And I'm sorry, but I'm betting your BBS people don't have 'mixed messages' as one of the things they're asking the workers to look out for."

These are all new thoughts, and they're coming so quickly I feel I'm struggling to keep up. "So, okay, let's say for the sake of argument you're right. You're saying behavior-based safety is just what, just wrong-headed from the start?"

He shakes his head. "I don't know. I'm not a safety guy, and I have to believe that if your consultants are such superstars, they must have some first-rate results to show for their efforts."

It was true, I reflected—everywhere they had worked, safety had improved. "So what are you saying?"

He shrugs, "I'm just spit-balling. I mean, I dunno, maybe they have good results which could be even better. All I'm saying is that if you focus on behavior as a cause, without focusing on where the behavior itself is coming from, you might be missing the big picture."

"You're saying that maybe BBS is too narrow in its focus."

He nods, "Could be. Yeah. Not wrong, per se, but not wholly correct either. Like, you know, Newton was right as far as he went. Einstein just went further."

I smile, "And you're Einstein?"

He laughs, "I think I'm more like Watson. 'Watson come here, clean up this mess!' "

The fried ice cream arrives and Jeff's eyes get as big as his smile. "Yes!" he digs in and points toward my side of the table. "You've got a spoon there, help yourself."

"I don't know, I've never had fried ice cream before…" He makes squawking chicken sounds and I laugh. "Okay, maybe just a bite." I spoon a bit of the concoction into my mouth. Cold, sweet, crunchy, totally unexpected and delicious.

He's watching me. "Good, huh?"

"Mmm!" I nod, and then it strikes me how this must look. An obviously over-forty woman sharing spoonfuls of ice cream with a hunky young man as they grin at one another. Time to remember this is a business lunch.

I straighten up, trying to rediscover the thread of the conversation. "Okay, so if BBS is somehow failing to tell the whole story, and if behavior is really just another outcome, then how do we go upstream far enough, what's the answer?"

"In-gway-shun!"

I can't help laughing. "I'm sorry, I don't have my ice cream interpreter with me, in English please?"

He laughs too, wiping his mouth and then enunciating with great care: "Integration."

I shrug, lost again, "I know you don't mean forced busing."

He shakes his head, "No. It's just the idea that every management process has to be aware of every other management process, and behave accordingly. It means that things like Quality and Safety and HR and everything else can't exist in their own little silos and interact with the rest of the company only on rare occasions. We need to interact with one another and be a part of one another's decision-making at all times."

"And then we'll live happily ever after?"

He smiles as though he's heard that one before. "Yeah, it sounds kinda fairy-tale, I know, but it's not some pipe dream of peace and harmony and everyone holding hands singing "Kumbaya," it's just good sense and it's good business. I mean, ISO 9001 only defines about ten total management processes. Integration says: 'Look, if safety is important, it needs to have a seat at all ten of those tables.' Instead of, you know, being at like the kids' table in the other room, away from the grown-ups at Thanksgiving."

I shake my head, "You're gonna have to give me an example."

"Okay, top of my head, Management Review, that's an important one of the ten processes, it's when Managers look over their key objectives and evaluate processes for effectiveness, right?"

"Right."

"It better be right, I memorized it before my last review." He grins, and continues, "So you tell me, where is safety located in that process?"

I shrug, "Where it oughta be, I guess. I mean, as Director of Safety, I do exactly that kind of review every quarter and we—"

He's shaking his head, "No, no, no, not your own reviews. I'm asking you where is safety located in the reviews conducted by all senior managers?"

"How should I know?" He sits back, smiling, and waiting. I get the idea the brightening bulb must be visible over my head to all the other diners. "Ohhhhh, okay, so you're saying I need to be a topic on everyone's management review agenda."

"Right. Integration."

"But why should that be? What's to talk about?"

He laughs and spreads his arms. "What's not to talk about? I mean, I don't know safety, but you must have metrics, you must have ongoing activities and achievements even when there's not some high-dollar consulting firm giving you plans, wouldn't it be smart to have the whole company pulling with you, wouldn't it make sense? I'll make you a bet, I'll bet the only time safety gets talked about by other managers is when there's been some kind of injury."

I give a half-hearted smile. "Well, if there hasn't been an injury, I say so and everyone claps."

"Hey, I like applause as much as the next guy, but it's not really helpful in this case. You're describing a situation in which there's only company-wide action when there's a negative outcome, and that's being purely reactive. Integration preaches the gospel of being proactive. Constant action, constant learning, constant improvement."

It makes sense from a purely logical point of view, but something in me doesn't trust this sweetness-and-light vision of things. "I hear what you're saying, but you know what I think? I think if you try this integration stuff in real life, you end up with ten or twelve cooks for every dish on the table, and I think dinner takes eight years to cook and when it finally gets to the table it's a mess. I mean, it sounds like you're saying everything should be done by committee, you know the old question?"

"What question?"

"What's a camel?"

He shakes his head, "I don't know."

"A camel is a horse built by committee."

He laughs, and nods his way toward another spoonful of ice cream as I sneak a tiny one for myself. "Okay, I hear you, I'm not saying our world has to turn into nonstop management meetings twenty-four-seven. But if we can begin from the assumption, and Gosh, I hope we can, that our senior managers are of at least average intelligence, doesn't it make sense we should all at least know what we're up to and have an opportunity to ask for feedback? Because Joanne, I'm gonna tell you a little secret about how easy integration could be."

"I'm all ears."

He spreads his arms to encompass the restaurant. "This. This lunch, this conversation. This is a small slice of how it works. Director of Quality and Director of Safety sitting down to chat. Bouncing ideas. Hey, you know what, here's one. Think about the semiannual Management Review. It's a big deal because it happens only twice a year, and how much time do you get at that meeting?"

"I'm usually a half-hour in the morning, nine to nine-thirty."

"Right, and I'm usually ten-thirty to eleven. A half-hour to talk about six months of safety, more even, your vision of the next six months. Don't you deserve more than a half-hour of this company's attention every six months?"

He's right. "You know…" I muse, "If I'm getting this integration thing right, that meeting oughta be an all-day thing, and we ought to all be present for everyone else's presentations."

He points at me, smiling, "Score! Yes! That's a great idea!"

"And," I continue, rolling with it, "It should be more than twice a year, it should at least be quarterly."

He's nodding, "You know why it's twice a year?"

"Why?"

"Because that's the ISO minimum requirement for compliance. Our company has decided how to review its management practices based not on its own sense of its own needs, but rather on some document published by a bunch of guys who don't even work here. I think we can do better."

He's right. We could do better. We ought to do better. "You know Jeff, I'm starting to get this. This is what the late safety guru Dan Petersen meant when he said, 'Safety is a by-product of how well an organization is managed.' "

The restaurant is emptying, and it seems less festive without so many patrons. I slump back into my chair, suddenly depressed. I shake my head slowly, and his eyebrows go up, "What? Too much lunch?"

My head is shaking on its own, "No, too little of everything else. Too little time."

"Whaddaya mean?"

"You say this lunch is integration, fine, but this lunch is only happening because Pillar is hoping to get a dossier of reasons to fire me. He's going to expect you to call him with your secret-agent super-spy report, and you'll say what, 'we had a very interesting discussion, and there are a lot of ideas worthy of further pursuit' or whatever, but what have we really accomplished? We discovered that my quarter million dollar consultants might be totally wrong, we discovered—"

"Not totally wrong, just not broad enough in their vision of—"

I ride over him, "And we discovered our company's fundamental philosophy of management isn't the best for maximizing positive outcomes, yippee, like in thirteen days I can take that to Pillar?"

"Joanne—"

"Hi, Mr. Pillar, here's my report…I have concluded that you and your bonus-whoring buddies need to do a top-down rethink of our management practices, and then you'll be happy about what I'm doing with safety—thank you for your time!"

My voice has gone up and I'm drawing looks from the closest patrons, but I don't really care. I can see by the stricken look on Jeff's face I've made my point. I take a breath and try to speak more calmly.

"It's not that I don't appreciate everything you've said, Jeff, it's all useful and it all makes sense and you're obviously an enormously intelligent guy and I wish we'd had this lunch a year ago, but right now I hear a ticking clock and it's saying, 'Twelve days and five hours…twelve days and four hours and fifty-nine minutes' and it's counting down my whole career, and I just don't know how I can use what we've said here today, you know?"

He's nodding, silent, and I can tell he's thinking as hard as he can and I'm feeling bad, as though I've scolded him for helping me. From behind me I hear "Joanne? Joanne Sanders?"

Who knows me here? I turn, and see a familiar stoop-shouldered man smiling at me and I leap to my feet, knocking my chair over behind me and not caring. "Doctor Pitz—'Doc'—oh my Heavens!" and then I'm hugging him in a fierce embrace and he's chuckling and hugging me back. After a second I step away from him, "You look great!"

"And you're a charming liar." He looks at Jeff quickly and I step back.

"I'm sorry—Jeff Snyder, this is Dr. B.F. Pitz."

Jeff's eyes are wide as he rises and holds out his hand to greet my friend. "I recognize you from your book jacket photo sir, it's a very great honor to meet you."

Doc's eyebrows rise at the flattery. "I should have been sitting at your table, where I apparently am both handsome and important—it's nice to meet you, Jeff."

I gesture to an empty chair, "Can you join us for a moment?"

He shakes his head, "I'm afraid not; my gracious hosts are waiting for me by the door." I follow his glance and see two young people looking hesitant. Doc continues, "They're my keepers, assigned to keep me out of trouble until my presentation tomorrow; I'm doing the keynote remarks for a conference at the University tomorrow, kind of my version of a book tour for 'Actively Caring for People Leadership'."

Uh-oh, caught, "I'm afraid I haven't gotten around to reading it yet, Doc, but I promise, it's on my list and—"

"I've read it three times!" Jeff blurts out, "I think it's brilliant, sir."

Doc gives a tiny bow and smiles again. "Joanne always had excellent taste in friends, Jeff, thank you." He glances at the door. "Those poor kids don't know what to do—I should go. Listen, do either of you want to come to the presentation tomorrow? I'd be happy to get your names on the list."

I look to Jeff. "I don't know, Doc, I'm kind of in the middle of a big hassle at—"

"We'd love to!" Jeff blurts again, his eyes shining. I'm amazed at the transformation in him—one minute he's the smoothly confident young manager, and the next minute he's like a fifteen-year-old girl meeting her favorite rock star.

I smile and shrug, "Okay, we'd love to."

Doc's smile broadens, "Good, good, and maybe after we can get a coffee and catch up? I'm sure you've got all kinds of stuff to tell me."

I laugh, "Yeah, like the fact I haven't been Sanders for a long time." I hold up my left hand and waggle my ring finger.

He laughs with me, "Perfect, yes, I need to hear everything, I hope I see you both there! Jeff, very nice to meet you…" another quick handshake with the mutely adoring Jeff and then he's shrugging on his coat and touching two fingers to his forehead in a quick salute, "Until tomorrow!"

We watch him leave and then Jeff is punching me on my arm. "That was B.F. Pitz. That was *the* B.F. Pitz! How do you know him? You're my hero!"

I laugh, "He was my mentor when I was an undergraduate. I did a lot of research for him and his graduate students, especially my senior year. He meant everything to me, he got me through some pretty tough jams with my studies. I adore him."

Jeff is shaking his head in disbelief, " 'I adore him,' right, the whole world practically adores him."

I can't help laughing, "You act like you just met Mick Jagger!"

He cocks his head in confusion, "Who's Mick Jagger?"

Oh Heavens, am I that old? I open my mouth to reply but then he grins, "Gotcha!"

"Very good, well played, yes, but Jeff, I don't know about that thing tomorrow."

"Are You Kidding Me? We have to go, we have to. Joanne, he's a genius!"

"I know perfectly well he's a genius, I only graduated because he's a genius, but I don't see how spending the day at a leadership seminar and then having coffee with an old friend is going to fix my problem, ticking clock, remember?"

Jeff scoffs, "Like you've got some other master scheme you were planning to execute?"

I start to speak, but stop short. He's right. I've got nothing. Jeff continues, "Look, just before you saw him, you were all depressed about the fact that little old me and little old you can't do anything to help you because your basic problem is that our leadership isn't doing things the way they ought to, okay, and then here comes your old friend, and suddenly you're happy again and—"

"Of course I'm happy to see an old friend who once saved my life, Jeff, but tha—"

"An old friend whose specialty is leadership, the very core of your problem, and he invites you to hear his latest thoughts on the subject, what on earth could keep you away?"

"I don't know, the fact that I can't imagine how it could help?"

"Can you imagine how it could hurt?" He's staring at me, and then he begins bouncing up and down in his chair. "Please, oh please! Can we go see the very smart man??"

I laugh, "Okay, fine, we'll go. Especially since you're buying me lunch."

"Well done, very smooth. Check, please!"

A few moments later as we're settling into his car, I notice him buckle his safety belt and I give an approving sound. "Good."

He looks over, "What's good?"

"You buckled up. You know, you didn't on the way over here."

"I did too!"

"Did not."

"Wow." He reflects for a second then asks, "Well, why didn't you say anything?"

"I figured it wasn't my business."

"Well," he says, turning his key, "From now on, you have my permission to tell me anytime you see me doing something stupid, okay?"

"Duly noted."

"Cause you know what?"

I look at him, curious, "What?"

"The only way we get you out of this jam is if we work together, and good manners be damned." He offers his hand, "Deal?"

My hopes were on target. He's an ally. I shake his hand, "Deal."

CHAPTER 5

"Success is never final and failure is never fatal. It is the courage to continue that counts."

—Winston Churchill

I **GET BACK FROM LUNCH** with my head whirling—between Jeff's insights and the pleasant surprise of seeing Doc, the rest of the workday feels stale and unimportant. It doesn't help that every conversation and every task is informed somehow by my sense of that ticking clock only I can hear: Thirteen days. Not even thirteen anymore, more like twelve and a fraction now. Tick-tock. When someone asks me about a detail for the following month, I want to laugh in their face, "What's the point? I'm not gonna be here anyway! Do whatever you want!"

Of course, I do have things to look forward to. Doc's lecture should at least be nostalgic if not immediately useful. It'll be great to catch up with him, and who knows, whatever he says might shed some sort of light on my predicament. There's also the pleasant feeling of a new ally in Jeff, and the thought that somehow, with his brain added to mine, we can find a way to surprise Pillar and keep me on the job I've earned with sweat and tears.

But the most immediate good thing on the horizon is my son's baseball game this afternoon. Matt is fifteen, he loves baseball the way most of us love breathing, and his team is undefeated (knock on wood). Adding to the excitement of today's game is the fact that his opponent is a team for which Matt's best friend, Tommy Owens, is the star pitcher. Tommy's an amazing athlete and has been a terror on the pitcher's mound since both kids were in grade school. Back then Matt started calling his friend "Tommy Gun" and now everyone in the league makes use of this all-too-appropriate nickname. Of course, both boys have been talking plenty of trash to each other in the days leading up to this afternoon's game; a lot of off-season bragging rights hinge on the outcome.

When four-thirty comes, I'm out of my chair like a shot, thrilled to be on my way to something which couldn't have less to do with work. I feel those familiar little-league mom butterflies in my stomach—there are times when I get so nervous before Matt's games I actually feel physically ill. It's not just the hope for a good outcome; it's also the feeling of powerlessness, my absolute and total inability to affect the outcome in any way. The kids are on their own, which is, of course, the not-so-secret dread of any mother. Some small corner of my mind tries to make a connection between the powerlessness I feel at ball games and my current situation at work, but I push these thoughts aside. This afternoon is not about me and my problems, it's about Matt.

On my way to the county Rec Center I stop for gas. As I watch the "Total Cost" numbers spinning like a slot machine, I glance around the station, idly observing my fellow petroleum slaves. I note the SUV with the three kids horsing around in the back, and I wonder whether that dad needs a second mortgage just to fill his tank. I note the elderly gentleman filling his hybrid, and I feel a glow of irrational pleasure. I always love seeing older people embracing new technologies. It's so easy to avoid the new, the strange, and it gets even easier the older you get, as anything different starts to feel like more and more of a risk. Hats off to you, old timer!

Then a deafening roar from behind makes me jump and whirl around. Eight or nine motorcycles are gliding into the station, gunning their engines for maximum racket. Every head in the place turns to look at them, which is of course exactly what they want. They're a scary looking bunch—their eyes are hidden behind sunglasses, plenty of leather and tattoos, and it would be almost cliché if you couldn't actually feel the engines in your stomach, insolently powerful. The lead rider dismounts, and as he turns to unscrew his gas cap, I note with some apprehension the logo on the back of his vest. These are Gypsy Jokers,

 and they're seriously bad news. The Hell's Angels might be more famous, but the Jokers are just as dangerous, perhaps more so for feeling as though they're somehow stuck in the Angels' shadow.

I glance at my pump; I've got maybe five more gallons to go. I look around and see that everyone has adopted a protective posture, eyes down, moving quickly. A moment ago our biggest problem had been the price of the gas we were pumping; I'm sure that now any of us would pay double just to be on our way.

I look at the lead rider again, and notice with horror that he's smoking, his lit cigarette not more than two feet from the flow of gasoline into his bike. A single errant spark is all it would take to turn this entire place into a barbecue pit.

Should I say something? I look around quickly to see if anyone else has noticed. The kids are still playing in the back of the SUV, oblivious to the sudden danger. Their dad seems keenly aware he's in the presence of outlaw bikers, but he doesn't seem to have noticed the lit cigarette. The hybrid owner is already in his car and moving away. I don't see any station employees anywhere. There's just me. And I'm paralyzed with indecision and fear—fear of fire and of explosions, but also fear of the biker himself. Do I really believe he'll do anything but laugh in my face if I come on like some sort of Den Mother?

To hell with this, I can't be here. I shut off my pump before my tank is full, twist the cap back on, and practically lunge into my car, starting it up and pulling away. I feel horribly selfish—I've looked after myself, but I haven't done anything for those three sweet kids, or their dad, or anyone else.

Was there anything I could have done? It's impossible to say. If I had tried to speak to the biker I might actually have made matters worse. All I know is once again, I'm feeling mired in a swampy mixture of uncertainty and fear, and making choices that feel like avoidance.

I'm the Director of Safety for a major manufacturing firm. I have a deep and personal commitment to helping people avoid harmful situations…but how deep does my commitment really go if I run away from any trouble that seems to threaten me personally? I am so sick of being afraid, of feeling like I'm playing dodgeball with a blindfold on. I'm sick of running away from things…

…but enough of that. I'm making too much of some jerk with a leather jacket. Breathe, Joanne. Matt's game. You're going to your son's baseball game, you're going to have fun with your family and forget all this stuff for a little while. Yes.

A few moments later I'm pulling into the Giles County Recreation Center. It's a beautifully groomed facility, with a swimming pool, biking and walking trails, soccer fields, jungle-gyms and covered picnic areas…but the gem at its heart is the four-diamond cluster devoted to baseball, each field with its own home-run depth for different age groups.

I quickly spot Keith's grinning face as he waves me over, and I pick my way up the aluminum bleachers to squeeze in between Keith and Jessica. She speaks a muffled, "Hi, Mom!" around the biggest hot dog I've ever seen. I look around for Matt and see that his team, the Giles County Generals, is already on the field, with Coach Casey hollering different situations to them as he lofts hits to different players. I watch Matt in center field, moving easily, smiling.

In the far dugout, I see Tommy and his team, the Rockets, going over their batting order. Tommy looks relaxed and confident, and again the butterflies swirl in my stomach. Can my boy and his teammates really stand up to the pitching power of the Tommy Gun? It's only a game but there's a part of me that's already sad either boy would ever have to lose to the other. There are times in the life of a little-league mom when what you want more than anything else is an unexpected thunderstorm…

But! Matt's been looking forward to this all week, and after all, he's the one who has to live with the outcome. Time to be supportive. The boys field one last pop-up and bring it in at a brisk trot, clustering around Coach Casey at their dugout, which is only a few yards away from our spot in the bleachers. This is the moment when the coach gives a little talk he calls his "Motivational Minute." Sometimes he uses the moment simply to tell a joke, if he thinks the team is wound too tight. Other times he tells them a story meant to help them focus on a particular aspect of the game they're about to play.

Today he starts with, "Okay, gentlemen, I wanna tell you about something historic that happened last week. Who can remind us of the three C's we talked about on Wednesday?"

Several of the boys raise their hands, and when the coach calls on Kevin Sprague he hops up and says, "Commitment, Competence, and Courage, Coach!"

Casey laughs, "That's four C's, Kev, but I'll let it slide." As the boys laugh, I'm smiling to myself. I'm not even sure what Coach Casey does in his "real" life, but this three-C's idea is an extension of scholarship by the leadership guru—Ken Blanchard. Blanchard wrote about something he called "situational

leadership" and he mentioned both Commitment and Competence, and the coach's addition of "Courage" seems like an intriguing idea. I re-focus on the story he's telling.

"Gentlemen, there's a college baseball team at the Oregon State University known as the Beavers. Now last week, the Beavers found themselves in Omaha, Nebraska, playing in the World Series of College Baseball. They'd never been there before, and it's a double elimination tournament, with brackets of teams working down until one team is the champion, okay? You have to lose twice to be out." The boys were all nodding, the format clear to them.

The coach continued, "So there they are, the Beavers from Oregon, their first World Series ever, first game, bam, they get hammered by Carolina. The Tar Heels beat 'em something like nine to three, pretty lopsided. It doesn't look good for the Beavers, right, but what the heck, they made it to the World Series, no other Oregon team had ever done that, they can be proud just to be there, right? Well, yes and no. That stuff was all true, but they weren't ready to leave yet. And they're in real trouble because now they have no margin for error. If they lose one more game, they're done.

"All the TV guys on ESPN and Fox kept talking about it as though Oregon was already gone. But a funny thing happened—the Oregon players must not have been paying much attention to ESPN because they just wouldn't leave. They kept winning. They won their second game, and then their third, and their fourth, and every day it got harder, pitchers are getting tired, hotel beds are lumpy, there's the pressure of knowing that one muffed fly ball could be the end…but they keep winning. They won seven games in a row, and suddenly, everyone else has lost twice and there's only one game between them and the championship…and it couldn't have been better if it had been a movie, 'cause you know who they have to play? The UNC Tar Heels—favorites to win the whole thing. The team that beat them in the beginning."

He pauses to let the boys ponder the situation, then he goes on. "The Beavers fell behind early. Carolina was playing like they were the Red Sox or something, as strong as any team you'll ever see…except the Beavers didn't quit. In a way, they'd been behind for the whole series, so being behind in this game didn't spook them. Carolina, on the other hand, had never been in real trouble and maybe they relaxed a little bit, because in the eighth inning the Beavers tied the game and then took a one-run lead and they never gave it back. They won the whole thing. Now someone tell me how the Beavers show us the three C's."

A kid I know only as Bobby says, "Well, Competence because they're even in the World Series, they have to be pretty good players."

Coach nods, "That's right. What about Commitment?"

Kevin pipes up again, "They never gave up, even when they lost their first game and even when they were behind in their last game, they stayed focused and kept playing."

Coach Casey smiles and points at Kevin, "Yes! Exactly! And what's last?"

The team responds in unison: "COURAGE!"

Their coach is now beaming positively, but I see Matt's hand creep into the air tentatively, and Coach Casey points to him, "Matt?"

Matt seems to have some trouble forming what he wants to ask, and I'm riveted watching the wrinkled forehead I know means he's thinking at a mile a minute. After a moment he says, "Coach, I know courage is a good thing…but where do you get it?"

The boys who have been looking at Matt now pivot to their coach, and I'm all ears myself. I'd personally love to know what shop might be offering a sale on Courage this week. Maybe I could keep a little in the car to help me in scenes like the one earlier at the gas station.

Coach Casey nods approvingly at the question and takes a moment to ponder his answer before he says, "I'll tell you where it comes from, Matt. And I want every one of you boys to listen to this. It comes from loving the game and your teammates more than you love yourself. Giving yourself totally to every moment of the game. This pitch. This swing. This throw. Loving every moment of the game, because if you do that the game will love you back, and you'll find out later you did things that only the bravest person in the world could have done. Love the game, gentlemen. Bring it in and lemme hear that one on three."

The boys rush to cluster around him, their right hands thrust into the center and as one they chant, "One! Two! Three! LOVE THE GAME!!" And with that, they charge to their places in the field, and we parents rise to our feet to applaud. I look at Keith who's clapping so hard I think he might break his hands, and I grin at how close all us parents are to storming the field and joining them. The Motivational Minute has definitely done its job.

FOUR INNINGS LATER some of the excitement has worn off. I know there are people in the world who can find drama in every pitch of a baseball game, who note whether a shortstop has taken one step too many to the left, and who have spirited debates about whether the coach might call for a squeeze play…but I'm afraid my appreciation doesn't run that deep. I want my son and his team to do well, and I know if he catches or hits the ball, that's good…but unless there's a lot of scoring I tend to lose some of my interest.

This game certainly has little in the way of hitting or scoring. Both teams' pitchers are doing very well, with Tommy Gun holding the edge—he's pitching a shutout, while his team, the Rockets, have managed to score twice. Matt has only batted once, and he managed to fight off a full count for several pitches until a Tommy-Gun special fastball got him out. I'm pretty sure he'll be up the next time his team is at bat, and as I watch him in the field, I wonder whether he's excited or nervous about facing his friend a second time.

I notice the left fielder glance at the scoreboard and it occurs to me this reflects a basic notion of human performance. The scoreboard lets the players know how they're doing, and allows them to make decisions and plans for the immediate future. It's a data point, and it's not so different from the way we're trying to use various kinds of feedback to improve human performance in the workplace, including behavior-based safety. Before I know it, I'm following this line of thought with more energy than I'm following the ball game. Leave work at the office, I know, and I actually smile inwardly at the notion I'm a performance junkie…but isn't that, at some level, the definition of commitment? When you never really stop working on something?

Next, I start to wonder how the feedback of the scoreboard is making itself felt in the players' decisions. As the inning data grow and time runs short, the team that's behind will become more desperate, perhaps trying things that might not have felt safe in the first inning, because they'll begin to feel as if they have no choice. Not so different from Sloan reaching up into that chute. It'll be the coach's job to remind them to play within themselves, worry only about the task at hand.

Meanwhile, the other team is winning, but vulnerable. They'll try to protect their lead. They'd love to add further successes in the form of runs, but they won't take unnecessary risks to do that. In fact, they may start to play too tightly, worried about the closeness of the game. They may stop playing to win, and instead start playing to not lose—to avoid failure. It strikes me pretty forcefully that this is what I've been doing lately: Avoiding trouble. Minimizing personal risk. Playing not to lose. Playing scared.

I'm jarred from this disturbing line of thought by a burst of applause from our bleachers as Matt's team makes the third out and they come trotting in for their next at-bat. Matt's going to be leading off, and I sit up, shaking off the thoughts about my own troubles and putting my attention squarely on my son and this next duel with his best friend, and for the moment his greatest nemesis—the dreaded Tommy Gun.

But a funny thing happens. Tommy seems to be feeling a little frustrated that his team can't add to their lead, and he tries to compensate by doing everything himself, hurling pitches with devastating speed. The only problem is, his frustration seems to be costing him his accuracy, and yes, the pitches are fast, but they're missing the plate. He walks Matt on four straight pitches, and as Matt trots to first base, he glances at his friend. God bless this kid, he got on base but he's worried about his friend.

Tommy's coach comes out to say a few words to him, and while I can't hear anything that's said, it's clear the coach is scolding the boy. Tommy nods grimly, and the coach gives him an obligatory-looking pat and then returns to the dugout. A kid named Bobby steps up to the plate, and Tommy's first pitch hits him right on the leg.

Tommy pivots away from the plate, looking skyward in total disgust with himself as Bobby limps toward first, rubbing the spot where the Tommy Gun hit him. It clearly wasn't an intentional plunk, and there are no hard feelings…except here comes Tommy's coach to the mound again, and this time he seems much angrier. Now everyone in the stands can hear him as he berates the poor kid for his error. A few words are lost, but big pieces come through loud and clear, pieces like "look like a damned loser!" and "no one's out here to watch you make an idiot out of yourself!" and "whole damned season is on the line!"

I can't believe what's happening. I know we women sometimes don't get the rough and tumble world of boys' sports, and there's an awful lot of behavior on the playing field which seems to me to be unnecessary or mean-spirited…but I've never heard anything like this. I can't imagine Coach Casey ever talking to any of his boys that way, and if he did you can believe I and many other parents would pull our kids off the team in a heartbeat.

I glance at Keith to see whether he's taking this the same way I am, and his jaw is set and his eyes are narrow, and I know he's furious. I glance around at the other parents and everyone is clearly disturbed by what they're hearing. Some seem embarrassed, looking down and squirming. Some are murmuring things to one another as they keep their eyes glued to the scene on the mound.

Lastly I check the boys on each team. Most of them are staring, open-mouthed, at this alleged grown-up behaving in such a juvenile fashion. I can't see Matt's eyes at second base, but I can read his body language, and he's either terribly upset or terribly angry or both. That's his best friend out there, and the kid made one mistake and now he's being carved into pieces in front of everyone.

My focus returns to Tommy and his coach. I feel a deep pang of empathy for the kid. After all, this isn't so different from the scene I went through in Pillar's office … except I took my lashes in private, not in broad daylight in front of friends and family. I also have quite a few more years of life to help cushion me against such indignities, and even with that experience I was still devastated by it. This poor kid has it way worse than I did. How on earth is he supposed to continue after this?

At length, his Coach seems to run out of venom, and spitting at Tommy's feet he says, "Get your head in the game and finish it!" and then stalks back to the dugout. As he gets near his team, they seem to shrink away from him, but I doubt he notices as he plops himself back onto the bench, glaring furiously outward.

On the mound, Tommy is staring at the ground, and I'm quite certain he is fighting tears. This is one of the very best pitchers in the entire league—there's already been talk of college scholarships—and in thirty seconds that jackass of a coach has robbed the kid of all his confidence—his sense of competence. Does he honestly believe humiliation and motivation are synonymous?

I can see Tommy draw a shuddering breath and dig in his feet, trying to capture the familiar rhythm he's coded into his muscles and bones summer after summer. I know he's on the other team, but I can't help silently rooting for him.

I have a feeling I'm not the only one. C'mon, Tommy, I'm thinking. Show that idiot what you can do.

As he winds up, I see his face is screwed into a mask of angry pain, and I just know the bullet coming out of the Tommy Gun this time is going to be moving faster than any pitch he's ever thrown before.

Our batter, a carrot-topped kid named Josh, is thinking the same thing. He begins stepping into his swing even as the ball is leaving Tommy's hand, gambling it'll be a fast ball down the middle. He's right. His bat connects with a deafening crack, and the ball heads toward the stratosphere. A home run with two men on base, and our team takes the lead.

There is some clapping and cheering from our side, but all of us feel sorry for Tommy, who must feel as though he's just lost the game for his team when in fact all he did was get derailed by a coach who ought to have known better. The three C's? Tommy came into the game with all three—loads of competence, the deepest possible commitment, and the courage to stand by himself on a lonely hill and face batter after batter with only his wits and his skill to help him.

But none of that matters when a selfish fool with power over you decides he'd like to blame you for his own troubles.

Tommy's coach has yelled at him to get off the mound, and Tommy is trudging, head down, to the dugout, to a seat as far from the coach as he can find. I can't blame him. He's a coach in name only—he has failed at every step of his job today. He hasn't motivated, he hasn't helped, and the only teaching he's done has been to set a negative example that some of us parents might be able to use in talking to our kids later tonight.

And I can tell, just by looking at his face, he's oblivious to all of this. He couldn't care less about the cost of his actions, he's not even aware of them—to him, these teenage kids aren't anything but objects in his own self-absorbed game, to be used and abused however he sees fit. He's done massive damage to Tommy and I would imagine to his entire team today, and he doesn't even care. No, it's worse than that—he doesn't even know.

If Coach Casey is right (and I think he is) about courage coming from love of the game, then Tommy's coach is the living antithesis of this idea—a grown man, so terrified of losing a simple game he loses himself in the process. Whatever love he might have for the game is overwhelmed by his fear of losing.

I wish I could say these things to Tommy in a way he would understand. I wish I could say it to that coach. For that matter, I wish I could say it to Pillar.

AFTER THE GAME, Keith has to run Jessica to a 4-H meeting, so Matt rides home with me. We're both terribly upset and worried about Tommy. Matt tries his cell phone but gets no answer, and I do my best to reassure him his friend will be fine. "Tommy's a tough kid," I remind him.

"Tougher than that fat jerk coach," Matt growls. I can see in his young face the exact set of his dad's jaw as he says this, and I have to fight back my smile. Like father, like son.

Matt continues, "Without Tommy they wouldn't have won any games this year! Why would that guy act like that?"

"I don't know, kiddo. Did your coach say anything about it to you boys after the game?" I ask curiously.

Matt shakes his head, "Nah. He just told us he was proud of us."

"So am I." I reach out to pat his leg, and he smiles, but the smile is short-lived, and he turns to look out the window.

"He's just so mean," he says, staring at the passing trees. "He's, you know, this big guy, and he's already in charge of the whole team. Why does he need to act like that?"

"He's just a bully, I guess," I answer.

Matt turns to me, surprised. "That's it," he says, nodding vigorously. "Exactly." There's a moment of quiet and then he says, "I guess I thought bullies were mostly in school, like, the older you got, the fewer of 'em you have to deal with."

I laugh softly, thinking again of Pillar. "You'd be surprised," I say.

He's clearly intrigued by this new label for Tommy's coach. "So that means this guy is really just a coward, right? I mean, you and dad always say bullies are just cowards trying to act tough because they're secretly afraid."

I can feel him watching my face as I process this question, and I can't help but agree. "That's right," I say.

"So that's like, the opposite of courage," he muses. "The three C's our coach talks about, that guy didn't look very competent, standing out there yelling at a kid … and I don't know how committed he could be, 'cause if he was really committed to his team he wouldn't treat em like that, and even if all he was committed to was winning, he still wouldn't wanna shake up his best pitcher like that. And zero courage, 'cause like we said, he's just a big stupid bully."

We're pulling into our driveway, and I can only shake my head. "I don't know, sweetie. I can't tell you what's in that man's head. All I know is if you're going to work with young people, you need to put them first. It's a job that requires compassion."

Matt smacks his fist into his palm, "That's it!"

I glance over at him, concerned, "That's what?"

He's grinning, "You just added a fourth C. Competence, Commitment, Courage…and Compassion! That's what makes our coach so much better than that other guy, 'cause he really cares about us. Hey, even Care is a c-word. Cool, huh?"

I'm smiling back, "Cool is a c-word too."

"Correct, Ha!"

We're both grinning at this new word game as we collect his equipment. "Clever," I answer.

We bounce c-words back and forth as we make our way into the house, but in the back of my mind I'm running through this new-and-improved list: Competence, Commitment, Courage, and Compassion. He's onto something, all right.

Now if only I could figure out where these things come from and how to always have plenty of all four at my fingertips.

CHAPTER 6

"Organizations learn only through individuals who learn."
—Peter Senge

THE NEXT DAY, JEFF AND I are a few hundred yards away from the Campus Convention Center when it becomes clear parking could be a greater problem than we had expected. The University hosting Dr. Pitz and the conference is truly gorgeous—beautifully groomed grounds, more "manicured" than "landscaped." I imagine hundreds of dedicated workers on their hands and knees each night trimming the grass to eighth-inch tolerances and vanishing before first light so the rest of world sees only the results and never the labor. The buildings are all ancient, dignified stone and the overall sense of importance is tangible.

But as we approach the Convention Center, the timeless dignity gives way to a more modern feeling of bustle, with cars and buses approaching from all directions, and the temporary signs guiding guests. There are clearly a lot of people at this thing.

We're forced to continue past the Convention Center itself, looking for any empty space that's remotely BMW-shaped. "This is why they keep the grounds so nice," Jeff jokes. "This way, no one has the guts to park on the grass when the lot is full."

Eventually we find an empty parking spot on the lane leading back to the main Quad. We walk-trot the two hundred yards back to the Center. We know we're a couple minutes late, and our hope that the crowd might have delayed the start doesn't seem to be holding up—there are no people outside or in the lobby as we approach. "I think we just officially became residents of the Standing-Room-Only section," I muse, and Jeff just quickens his pace another notch.

It's a good thing I run every morning, otherwise I'd be panting like an asthmatic by the time we actually reach the sign-in desk. A professionally pleasant hostess whose name tag says she's "Dawn" asks if she can help us. We give our names and she finds our packets and badges, and gestures us toward the main doors. "Don't worry," she assures us, "I don't think they've really started yet. Just sit anywhere you like."

We thank her and duck inside. It's big—at least a thousand seats—and quite full. Jeff spots two empty seats on the far side, toward the back, and we move quickly toward them, slipping quietly into place. Dawn was right, we haven't missed much of anything—a balding administrator is in the middle of some scripted introductory remarks. "Seems like a friendly crowd," Jeff murmurs.

I shake my head, "I couldn't do it even if they were all family. I don't know how anybody gets in front of a group this big, I'd be a deer in the headlights."

The introductory speaker is droning through his index cards. It occurs to me the live comedy shows on TV have the right idea, hiring a comedian to warm up the audience before the show starts. Why do these academic conferences insist on doing their best to put you to sleep before the thing even starts? Still, I catch some of the tidbits he's offering about Doc.

"…known this teacher, researcher, and scholar for many years, and have seen again and again how his research dramatically improves the ways in which people work with one another, to the benefit of not only themselves, but of the very society within which they labor.

"He has had a tremendous impact on leaders' behaviors and attitudes in work cultures worldwide. His research and scholarship exemplify the motto of this University—'*Ut Prosim*' or 'That I may serve.'"

As he continues, my mind wanders from him again. I notice the presence of two gray overhead projectors on the stage, and I have to smile. Doc obviously hasn't changed much. When I studied with him, he loved overhead projectors, and it's in perfect keeping with this character that he wouldn't have bothered to learn how to make a PowerPoint presentation or use any other newfangled technology. "If it ain't broke, don't fix it" was always a famous motto of his.

I smile at the thought of how his hosts must have received his request for the projectors. Can you imagine the looks of consternation on their faces when their honored guest eschewed their multi-media, surround-sound projection system? And then of course they'd had to dig around in the teaching-appliance graveyard and actually find two overhead projectors.

I notice the introductory speaker seems to be wrapping up, thank goodness. He has looked up from his cards and tucked them into the pocket of his tweed jacket, smiling in what might have been relief. "Well, I don't want to take any more of our speaker's valuable time. Please join me in welcoming Alumni Distinguished Professor—Dr. B.F. Pitz."

The applause is thunderous and long lasting. Dr. Pitz walks onto the stage, smiling at us, seeming half-pleased and half-embarrassed by the reception. His appearance isn't that different from my memories of college—he is dressed casually in a sport shirt, slacks, and tennis shoes. I remember thinking that those tennis shoes were an ostentatious affectation when I first saw him in a psychology class twenty-five years ago ("Check me out, kids, look how non-conformist I am!"). But now I know there's a simpler reason for them—they're comfortable, and he's got more important things than footwear on his mind.

He has aged, of course, looking far more distinguished with his gray hair nicely combed back. There's a lavaliere microphone clipped to his shirt, so he can move wherever his spirit takes him during his lecture. There's a podium at the corner of the stage, but I already know he won't use it—he paces back and forth across the stage between the two overhead projectors, animated by an infectious excitement. I can feel my mouth turning up in a smile at all of these familiar sights. It's nice to see that some things don't change.

He dives in, "Thank you, thanks for that, that's all very nice. Welcome. I'd like to start by telling you two stories.

"The first is about a fellow named Mark Snyder, a lifeguard in Middleton, Texas. A few years ago, young Mr. Snyder is watching as four young boys run near the edge of the city pool. The kids are playing tag, all around the pool and the surrounding area. They are obviously not complying with the "no running" signs posted throughout the area, but Mr. Snyder says nothing. At one point, a woman complains to him about the children's unruly behavior, but he ignores the issue.

"At some point in their game, little Joey Taylor is tagged 'it,' and he begins chasing the others. Running after his little brother Carson, a fast slippery little guy, Joey hits a really slick spot and goes flying—feet first. The back of his head cracks hard against the cement deck, right here on the occipital lobe. He is motionless on the cement. A few adults near the space where he has landed scream and jump up to help.

"Now our lifeguard Mark Snyder gets involved, but it's too late. By the time someone calls 911 and the emergency response team arrives at the pool, little Joey is having convulsions. The EMTs do all they can, but it doesn't matter. Joey Taylor is declared DOA at The Good Samaritan Hospital.

"Two weeks later, another tragedy occurs. Mark Snyder takes his own life in the aftermath of shame and guilt for not intervening to prevent Joey's tragic fall. Two deaths from one preventable incident."

The auditorium is pin-drop silent—in a matter of two minutes, we've moved light years from the hearty warmth of the welcome, and we now find ourselves in the darkness of real tragedy. I'm as riveted as anyone else, wondering where Doc will take us.

He continues, with a showman's intuitive understanding of the control he wields over his audience. "A few months later in Corvallis, Oregon, a woman named Thelma Thomas is driving along Highway 99. Thelma is seventy-two and an avid reader. When she isn't reading, she's involved in community service. She is a model citizen and a friend to everyone she meets.

"The day we join Thelma we're in the eleventh straight day of heavy rains across her area. There is excess water everywhere, and the wide ditch alongside Highway 99 is filled with four feet of water. It's still raining hard as Thelma hits the curve known as 'Horseshoe Bend.' She's traveling too fast for the conditions, and she loses control of her car on the wet slippery road. Thelma's car swerves and tumbles and rolls over three times before landing upside down in the water-filled ditch.

"About two minutes later, Robbie Moreland approaches Horseshoe Bend in his Arrowhead water-delivery truck, and he notices three cars pulled over. People are out of their cars looking off to the side. One person is pointing. He thinks it strange for people to be outside their cars in the middle of a pouring rain. So, he flips on his emergency flashers and pulls his delivery truck over to see what's up. He sees a car turned upside down in the water-filled ditch and immediately runs down to that car.

"He tries to get the door opened, but can't. He finds a rock and smashes the window on the driver's side which is already cracked from the crash. He then reaches in and gets a hold of Thelma, but she doesn't move. The safety belt is tight around her.

"Robbie quickly reaches into his pocket and takes out a knife. He then cuts the belt to free up Thelma's body. He maneuvers her through the broken window, doing his best to try and avoid cutting her, and brings her motionless body out onto the embankment next to the ditch.

"Thelma is not breathing; she's been under water for over two minutes.

Without delay, Robbie begins mouth-to-mouth resuscitation. After forty-five seconds which feel endless, Thelma's body shakes and water jolts out of her mouth. She coughs profusely while gasping for air. Robbie Moreland has just saved Thelma's life."

We're held rapt by this tale of courage, and it's clear the two stories are intended to show different sides of the same coin. Dangerous situations, one faced with heroism, the other with negligence leading to tragedy. Doc spreads his arms wide, asking us the central question: "What would you have done? Could you be the person who is supposed to be conscientious—paid to save lives— but says nothing while little Joey Taylor slips and dies? Or, are you more like Robbie Moreland, a person who one day happens upon an overturned vehicle and immediately rushes in to help while several onlookers do nothing?"

He moves to one of the overheads, fishing in a battered folder for a transparency while continuing. "A different way to ask this same question is, 'Are you a person who understands how important it is not just to care, but to actively care?'" He slaps a transparency onto the glass, flips the switch and the phrase "ACTIVELY CARING for PEOPLE" is projected in large, bold letters. He pauses for a moment and then continues. "We all like to think of ourselves as caring individuals. Indeed, all of us care about something, even if it's only ourselves. But caring isn't enough—do you act on your caring, do you have it within you to do something when the moment demands it?"

He pauses again to let the directness of this question filter through us. I can sense the audience wrestling, wanting to believe that yes, of course, they would be like the hero, they would never let someone die…but didn't that poor lifeguard think the same thing about himself until the critical moment came? Would we be any better?

Doc gives a reassuring chuckle that brings us back to the stage. "Relax, folks. It's a trick question. And it's a trick that's been fooling most of us throughout our lives—indeed, it's fooled mankind itself for centuries, maybe forever. The trick is the presumption there's a single trait which either resides within us or doesn't, something we may think of as "courage" or "heroism," and many believe this is a binary state—one either has the magic trait, or one does not."

He pauses to look at us, and it feels as if somehow he makes eye contact with each of us before he says, slowly "This…is…not…true."

His quiet passion has us on the edge of our seats, wanting to hear more, wanting to hear him reveal the secret. At length, he continues, "The fact of the matter is, our propensity to actively care—to act on our caring—is not the result of the presence or absence of one factor, but rather, it varies according to several factors. Which means our job—as humans on this planet and as people attending this lecture—is to identify these factors and learn how to influence them so we can all become more actively-caring people. So that we may, in fact, become a planet of heroes."

Jeff leans over to me to whisper, "Hero lessons? I'm in!" I nudge him with my elbow as Doc continues.

"By way of illustration, let's look at two more opportunities to make a difference. Suppose your fifteen-year-old daughter is mowing your front lawn in flip-flops. Would you go out and say something to her? Of course you would. You care about her and you would act on it. You wouldn't even think of this as significant, let alone heroism. You'd call it 'parenting.'

"Later that same day, you go to the grocery store and two streets away from your home you see a fifteen-year-old boy mowing his front lawn in bare feet. Will you stop and say something? I'm guessing not, because the probability of actively caring is far less here. You don't know this kid. He's not your responsibility. The relationship is not sufficient to trigger your threshold for actively caring…but isn't that just an excuse? Don't we have a moral responsibility to help others avoid danger, regardless of our relationship with them? Shouldn't seeing someone at risk activate a moral responsibility to correct them, to help keep them safe?

"Intellectually, I'm hoping most of you are saying, 'Yes, of course.' But I'm betting those aren't the only words in your head. You're also saying, 'In a perfect world, sure, but people don't want you in their business,' or maybe your self-talk is, 'I guess he's willing to accept the risk, on his head be it.' Of course, we all know if you hear later the kid lost a foot because of a lawn-mower injury, you'll feel sick to your stomach at the idea you could have helped but didn't. It's not on his head. Now it's on yours. You've experienced a failure of courage."

I'm flashing uncomfortably on the memory of my neighbor's daughter and the sight of her forlorn little VW on the roadside. I shake it off and re-focus on Doc, who is approaching his other projector.

"I spoke a moment ago about our mistaken belief that courage is a binary trait you either have or you don't, and how this is not the case. Let me disabuse you of another common misconception: We tend to think of courage as a broad-stroke quality, making itself felt in only the biggest moments—you know, rushing into burning buildings or throwing yourself on the hand grenade or whatever...but again, I have to say this is not true. Courage makes itself felt in a thousand small ways every day, whether you're saving a drowning woman or reminding a youngster to put on a pair of shoes. The leadership quality we think of as 'courage' varies as a function of two other qualities—competence and commitment." At this point, Doc has produced another transparency, which he places onto the second projector.

Three States Determine Performance.

"As commitment and competence rise, so does the state we call 'courage' become more likely. If you're committed to helping others but you lack the competence, then you're likely to be one of those persons standing at the roadside watching Thelma drown. If you're competent, but lack commitment, then you're probably going to be like the poor young lifeguard, who had all the training he needed to stop those boys from running, but didn't care enough to put a stop to their behavior. But—when competence and commitment are both present in abundance—whoosh!" and with a flourish, Doc continues the "courage" vector right off the projector and toward the heavens.

There's an appreciative laugh and he grows a bit quiet. "Actively Caring for People. Courage. Leadership. I want to encourage you to think of these things as being not only interrelated, but more importantly, I want you to begin thinking of them as behaviors. Leadership isn't a quality, it's a way of doing. Courage is doing. If you claim to care but don't do anything about it then you forfeit the right to that claim. People who actively care for people do things."

Again I'm flipping through the events of the last few days and feeling a creeping shame within me as I review all of the times I've had a chance to step up and act, but have chosen to lay back. I felt as though I had good reasons at each point, but now, listening to Doc—

"SO HOW!?"

His loud cry jolts me from my penitent self-examination. Yes! Tell me how!

He smiles, "I'm not going to pretend I have some magical, one-size-fits-all courage suit up here to show you. But I believe I have the next best thing. Research in the behavioral and social sciences has shown there are five basic conditions or states which are constantly shifting within you…and I've come to believe, after a great many studies, that we can influence these states in ourselves and others, with Actively Caring for People as the potential by-product of our efforts."

He pauses for emphasis. "Let me say this again: Research has shown we can absolutely influence the amount of courage in the world. We can generate it within ourselves and within the people around us, with the same certainty others apply to physics or to chemistry. When one mixes hydrogen and oxygen, the inevitable by-product is water. I'm going to teach you the same basic idea for cultivating actively-caring-for-people courage."

He returns to the first projector and replaces the "ACTIVELY CARING for PEOPLE" transparency with a diagram of a five-pointed star.

At each point is a simple term, like "self-esteem" and "belongingness"…and at the star's center, in capital letters, the single word "Courage."

Doc begins working his way around the points of the star, totally in his element, lost in the passion for the

Five Person States Influence Actively Caring.

Self-Efficacy
"I can do it"

Personal Control
"I am in control"

COURAGE

Optimism
"I expect the best"

Self-Esteem
"I care about myself"

Belongingness
"I care about my team"

message he's delivering. I remember these moments from my college days, too—the feeling that I wasn't in the presence of a mere professor, but instead a kind of missionary, a man driven by beliefs larger than himself whose excitement seems to lead everyone who hears him to the same inescapable conclusions.

"Each point represents one of the five conditions I spoke of, which I refer to as 'Person-States.' These five person-states won't be news to you, but you may never have thought of them as interacting in this way before. While competence and commitment are necessary for actively-caring-for-people courage, they are not sufficient. These person-states play a critical role.

"Self-esteem! That one's easy, right? How well do we think of ourselves. This isn't always totally within our power, even the biggest ego can be wounded by thoughtless criticism, and inflated even further by the simplest affirmation or praise.

"Belongingness! Do you belong? Sometimes that one's pretty easy—if you're at your family's Thanksgiving table, you probably feel as if you belong…but who among us hasn't been that restless fifteen-year-old who thinks the grown-ups are all idiots and that stuffing makes you fat?" There's a ripple of appreciative laughter, in which he freely joins.

"You see? Even at a family celebration, the sense of belonging can be more tenuous than you might suspect…and so how much more tenuous might it be at the workplace, or the community pool? The fact is we all belong to one big family, the family of humankind…but we don't always feel welcome at the table. It's our job to look around, and if we see that disaffected face, to say something simple, like 'I'm glad you can be here.' After a simple statement like that, even the calorie-counting fifteen-year-old is brought back into the fold with astonishing swiftness."

Jeff leans over to me again. "This guy's amazing," he murmurs, and I grin my agreement.

On stage, Doc is still blasting away. "Self-Efficacy! Which is a direct function of competence, just like on the vector diagram…" and he points toward the other projector's image still on its screen, continuing "…but self-efficacy is your belief in your competence, your faith that you can in fact perform a particular task. Do you believe you are skilled enough to do what you're attempting? We achieve self-efficacy through our competent efforts and when others recognize us for our worthwhile work.

"Personal Control! Who's running your life? Whose life are you trying to run? When people have power over you and are quick to remind you of that, your sense of personal control diminishes…and when you're allowed autonomy, doesn't it feel better? Don't you feel most capable when you're not the only one in charge but you know others trust you to be competent and in control of your part of the process?"

"Optimism! The glass is half full! Things will be okay! When you're having a bad day, does anything piss you off more than hearing this kind of crap?" The audience roars its laughter, and he continues. "But! But! But! Think about the people who are forever seeing the bright side of things—don't they in fact seem to have happier lives? If they see the glass as half full then isn't it really half full? Isn't that part of our resentment, because they seem somehow to actually work their cheery will and make it so? Well here's the news: Any of us can do that, for ourselves and for the people around us!

"Lastly! Look in the center!" With his grease pencil, Doc draws several sloppy circles around the center of the star. "Courage! People with high levels of self-esteem, of belongingness, of all of the five person-states, those competent and committed individuals can't help but show courage, they will take action in any situation, they will care, because their actively caring for people has been enabled and propelled by these states!"

He pauses for a minute to catch his breath. "I get a little excited," he says apologetically, sipping at a glass of water as the audience chuckles in appreciation. He wipes his mouth with his sleeve—no politics at all!—and then continues, a bit more quietly. "They're person-states, folks. They're not traits. They're not fixed and coded like height and hair color and left-handedness—they're states. They fluctuate. They change. They are subject to influences from within and without, for good and for ill. They can be raised by others. And they can be lowered."

Jeff leans over again and mutters, "Pillar" through gritted teeth and I nod, but I'm already way ahead of him. For these last moments I've been decidedly split in my focus—listening raptly to Doc and his incredibly logical formula, while viewing my own recent experiences through this astonishing lens. I'm remembering the dressing-down Pillar gave me, and I'm moving around the star as though it's a checklist.

Did Pillar lower my self-esteem? He certainly did—he called me a failure, and I was so surprised his words bit deeper than I might have expected. Did he lower my self-efficacy? Again, without question—competent people don't fail, so if I'm a failure I must lack competence. Personal control? He made certain to leave me with zero. Belongingness? He had threatened me with termination—how can you truly belong anywhere if they can dispose of you so easily, so callously? And optimism? That was a laugh. How could anyone have left that meeting with any feelings of optimism?

And sure enough, in the days which followed, I've not been myself. I've been hesitant. I've been fearful. I haven't acted. The neighbor girl's car. The punks at the gas station. Even the bullying coach at the baseball game. I've said nothing. Done nothing. And rationalized my inaction to myself. Apparently, I've allowed one man to transform me into a coward.

I become aware of Jeff's voice "…okay?" he's asking, and he looks concerned, "Joanne?"

I quickly dab my eyes, before they overflow, and I whisper, "I'm fine. I mean, not totally, but I'll tell you after."

And as my attention returns to the stage, I realize that "after" is almost here. How much time has passed? A minute? Ten? I've been so lost in my own shocked view of the recent past that I have no idea, but I can tell from Doc's tone he's summing up.

"…so, yes, it's probably true for my purposes, 'Actively Caring for People' and 'Courage' are synonymous. But my mission isn't to get us all using the same jargon. My mission is to help all of you understand that the five person-states are variable, we can change them, and when they're sufficiently elevated in one person, they begin having a ripple effect on the person-states of those nearby. It's almost as though it's radioactive or something."

He pauses for a moment, reflecting, and then cracks a smile. "Courage is Radioactive," he muses. "That might be an interesting title for my next paper. Get all the physicists to show up." The audience laughs as easily as if they were watching Jimmy Fallon. "But seriously, folks," he continues, "Isn't that the essence of leadership? Not simply to be your best but, more importantly, to enable those people you lead to be the best they can be?

"There's a school of thought among some managers which holds they must periodically lower the person-states of those around them, believing they will establish their authority most effectively if they occasionally lower your self-esteem or reduce your autonomy. This is both wrong and costly—it might help an insecure manager feel more powerful, but it has a net negative impact on the team and therefore on the quality of the work done by that team."

Jeff and I look at one another and mouth "Pillar" and almost crack up.

On stage, Doc is continuing the point, "When you actively care for people, it's not just evident and appreciated, it's contagious, and you end up nourishing the person-states of everyone around you, and they nourish everyone around them, coming right back to you. And this is the difference, not just between a successful person and an unsuccessful person, we're talking about the stuff that makes for successful enterprises, successful communities, and yeah, okay, I know how pie-in-the-sky this sounds, but why not be optimistic, right? A successful world. It's ours for the making. We need only to actively care for people.

"Like I said before, folks, there's no magic formula. Actively caring for people takes effort, and attention, and persistence. There is no quick-and-easy path to boundless and perpetual courage. Every person is different, every job is different, and every day is different. But if we make ourselves aware of the person-states, within ourselves and others, if we learn to make thinking about these states an automatic part of our decision-making, with their elevation an ongoing and continuous objective, we will be well on our way.

"We must pay attention to these five states in ourselves and in the people around us, and we must constantly challenge ourselves to maximize these states. Whether you're my neighbor, my colleague, my friend, or a total stranger, my obligation is the same: How shall I find the courage to actively care? How shall we help the people around us release the hero within?"

These final, simple questions ring through us for a moment of silence before Doc bows his head briefly and says simply, "Thank you for your attention."

The slight echo from his microphone hangs in the air for a fraction of time and then, as one, we rise to our feet, applauding and cheering so loudly his repeated "thank yous" don't have a chance, no matter how much they turn up the sound. Eventually he gives up and simply waves, smiling into our sea of unabashed appreciation.

CHAPTER 7

"Our lives begin to end the day we become silent about things that matter."
—Martin Luther King, Jr.

WE MAKE OUR WAY BACK through the cavernous Convention Center, re-tracing the steps of our hurried arrival but turning in the other direction once we're outside, making our way to a small coffee shop with outdoor seating. Doc had left word we should wait for him there, and I don't mind having a little extra time to collect my thoughts—before he arrives. His lecture hit on several points which feel critical to me and to the problems I'm up against. To be honest, I have no notion of how or even whether they might help me keep my position at the plant—Doc's points about courage feel somehow more fundamental, more important, than any mere job.

Jeff is equally enthused, talking non-stop about how simple and clear and obvious all of the material was, once viewed through the lens Doc so masterfully provided. "I mean, that's one of the definitions of art," he bubbles excitedly. "They say 'art' is anything that tells you something you already knew but didn't know you knew. You know?"

"I know."

A beat, and then we both laugh at this fractured sequence. Then Jeff's face becomes serious and he continues, carefully, "So, in there…during his lecture, there was a moment when you looked kind of upset…?"

I nod, "And I said I'd tell you later, remember."

He holds up his hands. "I'm not trying to pry or anything, if you don't wanna talk about it, then…"

"No, no, it's fine. It's just…well, it was a little bit like what you were just saying. I was realizing some things were so true, but I hadn't really recognized they were true until Doc shined his own special spotlight on them."

Jeff nods, waits, and then prods, "Liiiiike?"

I shrug, almost embarrassed at the obviousness of it. "It was that whole five-point star, the person-states. I went around that star point by point, and it was just so clear how Bob Pillar single-handedly lowered each of those states in me as casually as he might throw away a gum wrapper."

Jeff is trying to recall all five points of the star. "Self-Esteem… Belongingness…Self-Efficacy…Personal Control…and what, oh yeah,

Optimism. Sooooo, okay, yeah, Pillar the Killer pretty much went five for five there, didn't he?"

It's hard to keep my voice from being bitter. "He sure did."

Jeff is still obviously searching for the source of my seemingly sudden disquiet. "Sooo…I mean, I know how terrible that must have been, still is, but—"

"That's the problem. The 'still is' part of things, that's what got to me in there."

Jeff's eyes are direct and open to whatever is on my mind. "Tell me," is all he says, and I'm so grateful that for every Pillar, there's at least one Jeff.

So I tell him. I tell him about the way I've been somehow apart from myself ever since I walked out of Pillar's office. The way I've become suddenly fearful and careful, and choosing inaction and retreat instead of action. The ways I've tried to reassure myself I really do care, all the while avoiding the actions which would prove it, to the world and to myself. My neighbor's daughter, the motorcycle thugs, that horrible baseball coach. Everything.

Jeff tries to reassure me, "Joanne, I know how tempting it must be to start to see everything like some kind of failure, but you're not being fair to yourself. I mean, who in their right mind is going to march right up to the leader of an outlaw motorcycle gang and make some polite request that—"

I put up my hand, stopping him. "I've told myself that exact thing and dozens of things like it again and again when I'm lying awake at night, and they all make sense and they're all logical and rational and even true and you know what? It's still wrong. It's still not who I am. I like who I used to be, and I hate what I'm apparently turning into and I don't know what to do about it!"

My voice has risen and the quaver in it is audible to anyone within earshot, and I feel like an idiot, like some cliché damsel in distress who weeps at the slightest provocation and dammit, that's not me either. I take a deep breath and say simply, "I feel like I need help, only I have no idea what that help could be or how to get it."

"Do I hear an innocent citizen asking for help in her time of need?"

I turn quickly to see Doc standing there, smiling broadly…but his smile quickly dies as he realizes there's something truly amiss. He moves closer and pulls over a bench for himself, sitting as his concerned eyes study my face. "I'm sorry Joanne, that was dumb of me, I didn't realize—"

I wave him off, embarrassed. "No Doc, please, it's nothing, just, you know, a stupid thing at work, we were—"

Jeff cuts me off and says, very calmly, "She's not telling you the truth, sir, she's in trouble and we're trying to figure a way out of it for her, and neither of us are making much progress and I'm thinking it wouldn't be a bad idea for us to get your take on the situation."

He opens his arms, totally receptive, "I'll do anything within my power."

I'm not happy about this. I did not come here to drag my mentor into my stupid problems. "Jeff's exaggerating, Doc. It's nothing," I insist, shooting eye-daggers at Jeff, who seems totally unimpressed and unmoved by my obvious wishes on this issue; he actually makes a puppet-mouth gesture with his hands, as though I'm simply blathering. Ninety seconds ago I was so happy to count him as a friend, and now I want to punch him in his know-it-all face, but Doc saves him.

"Joanne. If I may claim the rights and authorities traditionally vested in distinguished professors and other luminaries, I say I'm quite sure you're full of shit." I can only gape at him; he's never spoken to me this way before! He continues, "Moreover, I'm quite sure your friend is right. I'd like to think you would do an old man the favor of letting him feel useful by listening to your troubles, so would you mind terribly letting me know exactly what the hell is going on?" His eyes remain fixed on mine, warm and encouraging, and suddenly my resistance is gone, and I want—no, I need—to tell him everything.

And so I do, from my drive into work that fateful morning and my certainty I was about to become the star of the company to my sudden and hateful shredding at Pillar's hands, and then to the disquiet and uncertainties which have haunted me since. Jeff chimes in with a few helpful details here and there, but it's basically me talking for about fifteen solid minutes, at the end of which Doc leans back in his chair, steepling his fingers together in that familiar way I know signals deep contemplation of a thorny problem. We wait like humble apprentices at the feet of some ancient master, and at length he speaks.

"Okay. Several things. One: I know you worry about your family and about how to provide for them, but you must realize you are absolutely in no long-term financial trouble. You know that, right?"

I shake my head, "I'm not sure what you mean."

He smiles, "I mean you live in an area that has a manufacturing density around the top three or four in the country, you're surrounded by major manufacturing facilities for over a dozen global companies, and in this age of ever-increasing liability, your skill set makes you so employable I'm a little surprised you don't constantly have an ear out for better opportunities."

I start to tell him I've always been happy where I am, and he holds up a hand. "I know, I know, you're in no hurry to go elsewhere and I understand that, I'm simply saying we can remove the 'what-am-I-gonna-do-for-an-income' factor from the equation. Fair enough?"

After a moment, I have to nod. He's right. There are lots of jobs for which I'm well-suited, and I know how lucky that makes me.

He nods with me and continues, "Okay, that's one. Two: I'm not convinced this Pillar fellow is actually going to fire you anyway."

I laugh dismissively, "Trust me, Doc, I was there. He looked at me like I was something he'd like to scrape off his shoe."

Doc shrugs and says, "You're right, I wasn't there. I'm sure he was angry with you and I'm sure he was doing whatever he thought was appropriate to motivate you to fix what he perceives is a major problem. But as you've explained, not only is it hard to prove there really is a problem—except for him and his pals losing their bonuses—but even if you *can* prove there's a problem, you can't prove there's a two-week solution available."

Jeff speaks up, "With all due respect sir, you're talking about logic—and I can tell you, Pillar's not thinking logically. He's letting his anger do the thinking for him. And as for him being serious about letting Joanne go, remember—I'm in this because he asked me to help him assemble a case for her dismissal."

"And have you done that?"

The simplicity of Doc's question stuns us both into silence. He waits for a moment and then continues. "The fact that he asked you to do this service means he himself isn't totally sure of his footing. And I daresay you've neither done nor will do anything to increase his comfort in this area. I'm not saying he can't fire you, I'm not saying he won't fire you. I'm only saying I'm not convinced—and even if he does it, I refer you again to point one, okay?"

We both nod.

He continues, "Three: Given points one and two, the real issue here isn't you maybe getting fired or not, maybe getting another job or not. It's about your person-states getting severely diminished by a hostile, external force. You recognize you've been depleted, and therefore you need to learn how to renew all five states and restore them to their proper high levels."

Jeff speaks up again, "Actually, Doc this is the one question I felt your lecture didn't cover as well as I would have liked." He realizes that both Doc and I are looking at him, and the silence seems to build some sort of pressure, pushing him to hastily add, "With all due respect of course, I don't mean to, what I'm saying, I mean, you were awesome, I just, you know, wasn't…um…I didn't get that." Another beat, after which he contritely adds, "Sir."

After another moment of silence both Doc and I burst into laughter, and Jeff smiles uncertainly, pleased to see he has avoided offending the Great and Powerful Pitz, but still not sure of his footing.

"Cookie Cutter time," I say, and Doc is nodding as he continues chuckling.

Jeff looks back and forth between us, "Cookie Cutter?"

I lean in to pat Jeff on the arm, "Don't worry Jeff. This is an old, old thing with Doc and his research. He tends to focus his attention on identifying various aspects of behavior and showing connections which might not have been recognized before, and armed with relevant data, points out the areas in which improvements can be made."

Jeff's not satisfied. "I hear a 'but' somewhere in there," he observes.

"Indeed you do," Doc nods. "And it goes like this: I can identify behavioral trends and connections, and a range of things to which workers and leaders need to pay closer attention…but: There are no one-size-fits-all formulas for instant correction. No simple, pre-packaged solutions."

"No cookie cutters," I fill in.

"Exactly," Doc continues, "Many people who make a living as consultants for various management and leadership techniques tend to offer nothing but cookie-cutter solutions—nice and tidy catch phrases and empty acronyms that look great on a poster but have astonishingly little value in terms of real-world application. I actually had to fight pretty hard to avoid entitling the lecture you saw today with one of those cutie-pie acronyms. A colleague of mine was pushing me to call it ACT, to stand for Actively Caring Today! I wanted to vomit."

Jeff looks uncertain, "At the risk of furthering your nausea, sir, I don't see what's so bad about that title, it sums up your message, it's punchy, it's—"

"What's wrong is that I'm not selling sneakers or breakfast cereal," Dr. Pitz cuts him off gently. "Yes, it's catchy, it's punchy, it's even accurate, as far as it goes, but it's too simple-minded. The subject is human behavior and the complex ways in which our interactions with one another can affect one another, and the ways in which we can work to manage those interactions to our mutual benefit. This isn't a sugar cookie, and a cookie-cutter formula would be, at best, overly simple, and at worst be deceptive and fraudulent."

Jeff is nodding, and I can see he's losing his sense of intimidation and engaging the deeper issues. "Okay then, so we're back to the basic question of 'how.' You've identified these person-states, you've demonstrated their interrelatedness, you've made a strong case for the ways in which their elevation generates what we think of as courage and leadership. It's not a cookie, fine, it's a five-course meal, fair enough. So tell us, Dr. Pitz—what's the recipe for this particular feast?"

Doc leans back and laughs, "Very good, Jeff, I like that one, I'm gonna steal it for the next time I give this talk. And your question is not a new one, believe me, so let me ask you one, a hypothetical: Suppose you have a friend whose marriage is going through a rough spot. Your friend confides in you; he tells you things are bad, he tells you he feels as though his wife has no idea what's important to him. What advice do you give?"

Jeff answers slowly, as though wary of some trap, "Well…I mean, I guess the very first thing I would say is, 'Have you bothered to tell her what's important to you?' and then go from there."

Doc claps and smiles, "Bravo. You'd advise the two people to actually speak and listen to one another."

Jeff looks at me, and I smile encouragement at him. "Yes, of course."

Doc leans in and asks, "You wouldn't urge your friend to follow the new five-step path toward enlightenment espoused by best-selling therapist, Dr. Feelbetter, the one who uses the acronym LOVE to direct you to Listen, Own, Value, and Empathize?"

Jeff shakes his head incredulously, "I wouldn't even know what that means."

Doc shrugs, "You could buy the book, couldn't you?"

"Well…yeah, I guess, but I don't need a book to explain that two people should start helping one another with simple, heartfelt communication."

Dr. Pitz slaps his hand on the table, startling us both. "There it is! Communication. The big C. Not 'Cookie Cutter'—those are the evil C's. You'd urge your friend and his wife to work harder at communicating, which is the fundamental basis for health and growth in all relationships.

"My work doesn't really recommend anything different. If you want to learn how your workplace affects the person-states of the workers within it, you know what the silver bullet to that problem is? Ya ask 'em. For instance you ask 'em, "Can you tell me one thing that's happened in the last few months that increased your sense of belongingness in our company? Can you tell me one thing that's happened to decrease that sense? And then you should ask, 'Is there anything we can do, individually or as a matter of company policy, which would help to increase your sense of belongingness?' "

I can feel myself nodding, "That's leadership right there. Checking in with your people, finding out where they are and finding out what you can do to help them if they're not where we need them to be."

"Exactly, Jo," Doc glances at me approvingly. "Leaders enable. And one of the things a smart leader will enable is this same Q and A process, moving in both directions."

"And the leader has to actively listen to what's being said. Not just take notes and pretend to be sympathetic," Jeff adds.

Doc is leaning in, excited as always to be discussing his favorite topic. "Yes, exactly, it requires empathy. You might claim to care, you might truly care, but if you can't put yourself in the other person's shoes, you won't ever make real headway in helping them make a difference."

"Compassion!" I blurt out, and both men look at me. I smile self-consciously but continue, "Compassion. My son and I were just having this exact conversation, after that horrible coach I told you about. We decided there can be no real courage without compassion, without acting on the empathy you feel for the people around you."

"And maybe," says Jeff, "it's another of those feedback loops—what I mean is, maybe the more invested you are in another person's states, the more compassionate you'll be, and the more compassionate you are, the better positioned you are to elevate those person-states in the other person as well as in yourself. Maybe the inside of your star needs to have both of those words—courage and compassion."

Doc is staring at Jeff and after a moment he says, "You're hired," and we all burst into laughter. Then he continues, "Seriously, Jeff, that's very, very good. I think you're onto something."

Jeff smiles wryly, "Well, maybe we'll both be knocking on your door for jobs if we can't crack this Pillar problem."

"Yes, the Pillar problem," says Doc, "We'd drifted away from that a little bit."

"I wish I could drift away from it a lot," I grumble, but Doc has a faraway, musing look.

"I wonder," he says into space, "Where does the compassion idea fit into that mess?"

Jeff snorts, "Compassion? The man wouldn't know compassion if you painted it on a ten-foot sign and dropped it on his head—which, by the way, is duty I'd volunteer for."

"Right," I say, laughing, "We could just have him bumped off."

Dr. Pitz is frowning at us, and it's amazing what a time machine that frown is—I'm suddenly an undergrad again, caught passing notes during his lecture. "If I thought either of you really believed that, this conversation would be over."

"Oh come on Doc," I say, rolling my eyes, "I think you know me well enough to know I'm not likely to do a Google search for BumpOffYourBoss.com, right?"

Doc shakes his head, "I'm not talking about that," he says sternly. "I'm talking about how ridiculous it is for the two of you to sit here and say another human being doesn't have the capacity for compassion."

I can't tell whether he's defending me or defending himself or both, but Jeff leans right in and says, "I beg your pardon, Dr. Pitz. Until you've sat in this man's office and listened to the kind of bile he's capable of spewing, I'm not sure you should take a tone with us about whether we know what we're talking about."

Doc sits very still for a moment, and Jeff holds his position, and it's almost like watching a game of chicken. Eventually, Doc says slowly, "I have zero doubt the gentleman is an angry person and his anger has had a powerful and negative impact on you both. If you'd prefer to leap to the simple and totally unhelpful endgame of hating him, then fine, that's your decision. What I'm saying is I do not believe there's a human being on this planet who isn't susceptible to compassion, and who isn't capable of it himself. And what I find interesting, Jeff, is when I asked the question about compassion, you assumed I was talking about Mr. Pillar, but I wasn't. I was talking about you two."

This catches both of us off guard, and he can feel our surprise. He continues, "This notion of compassionate courage is a powerful one, and it speaks to a distinction I make quite often—the distinction between physical courage and moral courage. Physical courage is one's willingness to face discomfort, even injury or death, because one's caring is greater than one's fear. Maybe you're the only compatible donor of a kidney or bone marrow for a loved one, and so you agree to undergo painful and threatening procedures. It's courageous, but it's not the same as moral courage.

"Moral courage is what's required when our convictions are under attack, when sticking up for what we believe might lead to an uncomfortable confrontation. I guess comfort is the key—when the stakes are physical discomfort, action requires one kind of courage. When the stakes are emotional discomfort, which many of us find more frightening, then moral courage is required.

"And what I'm asking you is, since you've both agreed that compassion is necessary and good, do you have the moral courage to show compassion for someone like this Pillar fellow? Can you find within yourself the empathy necessary to sincerely communicate with him?"

The question hangs over our table, and for some reason, it frightens me… and I realize it frightens me because deep down, I know he's correct. I can feel my head beginning to shake minutely, as some ancient animal part of me tries to reject the difficulty of what Doc is proposing.

He leans closer, "I know I sound like some self-satisfied guru on the mountaintop, telling you to love your neighbor when you're the one with everything at stake, and then I get to fly first class and go home, far away from all this. But Joanne, you know I'm right." He glances at Jeff. "Jeff knows it, too."

He sits back again, "You both know it's right because you're both good people. Look, this moment we're having is as old as heroism itself. If you look at all the hero stories which have been told over the many thousands of years, across all times and cultures, you find that the hero undergoes a difficult journey, and when the journey is at its most difficult point, the hero encounters a person of wisdom and power.

Then the hero thinks, 'Oh, good, this person will give me what I need to defeat the dragon or the witch or whatever,' and then this person of wisdom tells the hero something he or she already knows, but has simply lost track of. At this point, our hero finds the courage to go forth and complete the journey."

I want so desperately to not become emotional, but I have trouble controlling my voice as I say, "But Doc, that's my problem, that's been my problem these last few days—I know I'm supposed to have courage, but I don't, I can't find it. I used to have it, I used to know where to find it, it was always right in the center of me where I needed it to be, and now it's gone, that space is empty, and as stupid as it sounds I think it's because Bob Pillar took it from me."

Of all possible reactions, the big grin on Doc's face is the one I expected least…but there it is, warm and bright. "That's right," he says. "Bob Pillar took your courage. So you know what you gotta do?"

Jeff and I are both staring, waiting. We shake our heads, and Doc leans in and says, with quiet intensity, "You gotta go right up to him…and take it back."

CHAPTER 8

"It is one of the most beautiful compensations of this life that no man can sincerely try to help another without helping himself."
—Ralph Waldo Emerson

ON THE RIDE BACK TO the office, Jeff and I make small talk about the remainder of our day (so odd to think we have normal, everyday tasks awaiting us), and about the weather and about how many bad drivers there seem to be nowadays and anything—anything, except the unspoken question which hangs in the air between us.

At length, the suspense becomes too great for him, and Jeff asks, with a note of forced casualness, "So how do you plan to go about it?"

Of course he's asking about Doc's final statement, that I must go to Pillar and somehow reclaim my courage. Easy to say, harder to imagine, harder yet to actually do. In the moment, it sounds so obvious and straightforward—yes, of course this is what I must do. But now, in the car, the thought of it is both daunting and vague. I know the task is frightening, and I'm not even quite sure what it entails. It's not as though I'll be able to walk into his office, find a little bottle marked "Joanne's Courage" and pluck it off the shelf and make myself whole again. It's just not that simple.

Or is it?

Jeff's question still hangs in the air. "I'm not sure," I respond, idly watching the passing backyards of the houses at the freeway's edge. What are their lives like, I wonder, imagining a simplicity I feel myself envying?

Stop it, Joanne. Enough pity. Action.

"I know Doc was basically recommending a confrontation," I muse, thinking aloud, "I mean, it's clear he thinks I should go back into Pillar's office and let him know where I stand."

"Yeah, but what do you think?" Jeff asks carefully, his eyes on the road.

I sigh, "I think he's right. I mean, I know he's right, but my problem is that I'm not sure where I stand."

Jeff laughs, "That's simple. You stand for you."

I ponder this. "I stand for me. Meaning, I stand for my efforts, all the work I've done on the company's behalf…and more, I stand for myself, for my humanity, and for the fact that no one, from the highest boss to the humblest hourly temp worker, deserves to be treated the way he's treated me."

"Exactly," Jeff nods, clearly pleased with my answer.

"Yeah, but so what?" I shoot back exasperatedly. "I stand for myself, la-di-dah. What happens when he just stares at me and then says, 'I'm a busy man; you can go now.' "

Jeff thinks for a moment before saying, "You refuse."

"I refuse?"

He nods again, building the scene in his mind and clearly enjoying it. "Absolutely. You say, 'No sir, I won't leave. You've given me a task and I'm here to report on my progress to date and to tell you that you won't receive the benefit of my efforts until you agree to treat me like a human being instead of like some disobedient lawn mower that won't start.' "

I cough out a one-syllable sound that might be a laugh. "I like the sound of all of that except for the part about me having some progress to report."

Jeff risks a glance at me before his eyes return to the road and in that half-second I see surprise on his face. "You don't think you have any progress to report?"

I think for a moment. I've learned that behavior-based safety doesn't address some of the primary contributors to at-risk behavior, because behavior itself is an outcome of other, prior circumstances—things like environmental conditions, and the person-states of the workers involved, even the management systems in which those workers are asked to function. To truly improve the behavior, it's these preconditions we need to address, not just the behaviors they generate.

Furthermore, endowing workers and management with an understanding of Doc's five person-states can enable the kind of worker involvement we need if we want to reveal and refine these conditions. That's what it's going to take if we want to eliminate at-risk behavior.

This simple articulation of the lessons of the last seventy-two hours takes me by surprise, and the sound which comes out this time is more obviously laughter, the laughter of pleasant surprise. "I take it back," I say. "Between your support and Doc's brand of wisdom, I guess I do have something worth reporting. I think we have to design new processes that leave BBS behind and move us ahead into the Actively Caring for People arena Doc was talking about."

"Good," says Jeff, sounding like a teacher whose student has just done a good job with a tough problem.

But I continue to fret, "I just don't know whether Pillar will listen."

Jeff shrugs, "That's out of your hands. You can't control everything; you can only control your own actions, your own choices. And this is the right choice."

Right then is when I make a decision which feels more like a realization than a choice: "You're coming with me," I say.

He looks at me again and I can see the conscious act of will it takes to return his eyes to the road as he sputters, "Me? I, no, why would, no, that wouldn't be—"

"Jeff," I cut him off. "You've been a vital part of this entire process. I know in my bones I wouldn't have gotten this far without your help."

"And this is how you thank me, by ambushing me and dragging me into this—this—this thing?"

The sight of the cool Jeff rattled is amusing to me. I strive for a light tone. "You'd be accompanying me to a kind of duel; just think of yourself as being my second."

His tone does not mirror the lightness of mine. He's obviously trying to sound grave and authoritative. "Joanne, I understand confronting Pillar is frightening to you, but I think that's all the more reason to—"

"Oh, stop it!" I wave his efforts away as though they were a cloud of gnats around my face. "Yes, it's frightening. It's frightening to me and it's frightening to you, too, and that's why you're acting like such a wuss."

"I am not acting li—"

"Listen to me," I say intently, riding over him. "You're already in this thing, Pillar put you here, and no matter what happens when I meet with him, he's gonna want to meet with you next. Doc already said he doubts you're going to give him the report he wants you to give, so how do you imagine that scene will go?"

Jeff is silent; this obviously had not occurred to him. I press my advantage, "So the only question is how you'd like to see him—alone, letting him know you can't be of any help to him, or with me, both of us offering assistance as long as he remembers to treat us like human beings?"

He remains silent, mulling these options, and I soften my tone. "I need you there, Jeff. Yes, I think it would be better for you, too, but I'd be lying if I said that was my main reason for saying all of this. The bottom line is I'll be more comfortable if I can face him with you. Will you do that for me?"

After a beat he gives an enormous, exasperated sigh. "Why do all women know that trick, the do-it-for-me trick, like any man could ever say 'No' when a woman does that? No, no, don't even bother getting all indignant-feminist with me; you know it's true. I'll go. It's fine. You're right."

I settle back into the soft leather seat, "See? You're already behaving more compassionately."

"Yeah," he mutters, "and you're being a cruelly manipulative she-devil." I laugh out loud, and he joins me, and I allow myself the briefest glimmer of hope that maybe, just maybe, this could all work out.

LATER THAT NIGHT, I tell Keith about everything that's happened—Doc's lecture, our talk afterward, and my decision for Jeff and me to go and confront Pillar.

"So," I say when I've finished, "Whaddaya think?"

Keith has the faraway look in his eyes that means he's pondering something deeply. He used to play a lot of chess when we first dated, and I actually watched him play in a tournament one weekend years ago. It was far from riveting, and I remember being thrilled I'd had the foresight to bring a trashy novel...but I also remember this same look in his eyes when he studied the board and tried to imagine how it would look several moves later. I've learned not to press him to talk when he has this look. He might answer, but he won't even remember what he said later. So I simply wait.

After a short time he says, "What I think is, it's the only move you have. What are your options? Wait until the two weeks are up and then go in and try the same thing, but you'll have lost the element of surprise. Also, every day that goes by is a day in which he might do something himself that makes things more difficult—like hiring a replacement for you."

I nod, listening carefully. I hadn't even thought of this angle, but it's nice to see it works in support of my decision.

Keith continues, ticking off logic points on his fingers, "Two, I agree with what your old professor said, you don't really need to worry about negative consequences in terms of your market value. There are other employers out there who would welcome you with open arms, so you can at least act as though you have nothing to lose.

Three, the essence of your message is nothing but true—you've found a way to improve things, but you won't be able to implement your ideas until he decides to treat you with the respect you deserve. You're not demanding access to the company jet; you're simply requiring that he treat you like a person. I think it's the right thing to do. So when will you do it?"

I sigh, "I wish I could do it right this second, but since that's out of the question, I'll try tomorrow to make an appointment for his first open slot. I'll probably see him day after tomorrow."

"What do you do between now and then?" Keith asks.

"I don't know," I shrug, "Get nervous, I guess."

"Welllll…" Keith says slowly, "I'm sure this is just the ex-jock clinging to what he knows best, but dontcha think maybe you oughta practice? Get ready?"

I hadn't thought of this, and even hearing it doesn't ring any loud bells of approval. Practice for a conversation? "What do you mean?" I ask.

Keith leans in, excited to be contributing something, happy to be on my team. "Okay, look," he starts, "Pillar's been a real jackass to you, but you're basically going in saying, 'I'm willing to wipe the slate clean if you are,' right?"

"Right," I agree.

"Okay, and your agenda is to demand the respect you deserve, but always with compassion and never with anger, right? Don't turn to the dark side and all that, right?"

"That's right."

"Well, I don't know about you, but if it were me I could make myself all those promises and then when I'm in the room with him, the first derogatory thing out of his mouth would have me seeing red and forgetting all of my well-laid plans in a New York minute."

I nod. He's right. If Pillar returns to the track he was on in our previous meeting, I'm liable to just blow up at him. "That sounds about right," I say, "and you're saying I could do something to avoid that?"

"Sure," Keith is nodding, excited, "You practice. You get ready for it by practicing, like you're an actor rehearsing a play."

I laugh, "I have a hunch Pillar's gonna be working from a different script."

"Right," says Keith, "and that's why you have to practice, so you can bring him back to your script. Like, for instance, suppose he says, 'How can you come in here saying BBS is wrong after we spent so much time and money with those consultants because you said this was the right thing to do?'"

I think for a moment and Keith says, "See? He's not going to give you that much time to think. You have to have an answer ready."

"Okay, I get it," I respond, thinking quickly. "I would say something like, 'Mr. Pillar, we're talking about an area of behavioral science that's still evolving, and the advice I gave you at that time was the best thinking available on the subject. There are now some exciting new ideas I think would be of great help to us. After all, sir, there was a time when the smartest people in the world knew without question the sun circled the earth. We learned better, and that's how science works. If we cling to a particular way of doing things just because we used to think it was right, every one of our competitors will pass us like we're standing still.' "

Keith claps, "Bravo! Perfect! And especially the part at the end where you appealed to his competitiveness."

I grin, "You liked that one, huh?"

"I did. Okay, now, what if he says…"

We continue in this vein for over an hour, role-playing with Keith sometimes being Pillar and sometimes being me. At a couple of points Keith makes some useful catches, "That was pretty snippy, babe. I mean, I can't blame you, if it were me, I'd be all about ripping the guy's head off, but you say you want to do this without any kind of anger, so…"

I agree quickly. I don't want the meeting to turn into a hostility contest, especially since I could never win something like that anyway.

We continue to practice. It's useful, of course, but there's also something much deeper than its obvious utility. It's a living, breathing example of the partnership which exists so strongly between Keith and me. At one point, when he leaves to freshen our drinks, I reflect on the notion that here, in my home, all of my person-states are off-the-charts high, and Keith is a huge part of why.

When he returns and hands me my drink, I pull his head down close to me and give him a long, lingering kiss. He smiles in surprise. "Wow. What was that for?"

"For being so perfect," I say, holding his gaze.

He laughs, "Aw shucks, ma'am, just doing my job."

My hand is still on the back of his neck, "And a very good job you do, too."

"You know," he says softly, "if you keep this up, I don't think we're gonna get much further with your practice."

I smile, "We've got nothing but time, coach."

THE NEXT DAY PASSES in a kind of blur. I attend the usual shift-change meeting, deal with several run-of-the-mill administrative chores (setting time to review the BBS coaching schedule, approving the behavioral checklists for data processing, offering suggestions for the creation of some new signage on the plant floor, a dozen similar things), and for each, I find myself wondering whether I'll actually be around to see them reach fruition.

I also call Barbara St. Claire to schedule the first available time to meet with Pillar, and sure enough, tomorrow is his first opening. She sets us for ten o'clock, courteous and cool as ever, never letting on that as far as anyone can tell, I'm scheduling my own appointment for the guillotine. I don't mention that Jeff will be with me. Better to have a card or two up my own sleeve.

That afternoon I wander across the building to give Jeff the news. He's on the phone, but he waves me into the office, closing the door behind me and rolling his eyes clownishly to let me know how uninterested he is in his call. Eventually he's able to end it, and he hangs up with a theatrically large sigh. "Why can't some people tell when a conversation is over?" he asks.

I grin at him, "They just love you so much they can't bear to hang up the phone."

"Yeah, lucky me. What's up?"

I give him the news, not only about our meeting time but about my conversation with Keith last night and the role-playing we did to help me prepare.

"That's good," Jeff states. "Get yourself focused; be sure of your footing. Have you thought about how to respond if he asks you how you can be so sure the AC4P approach is better than BBS? Is there any literature to back you up?"

It's a good question, and we hit the Internet, discovering several articles (quite a few by Doc, of course) which support this thinking. Before I know it, Jeff and I are doing some role-playing of our own, and sometimes I play Pillar asking Jeff what he thinks of Joanne's ideas. He's very flattering and before long we're into an exaggerated escalation of praise until we're each taking turns telling Pillar the other should be named president of the entire company, of all companies in our industry, of every nation on earth.

Jeff's smile fades first and then he says, "There's one question I think he's going to ask that we haven't covered yet."

"What's that?" I ask, worried about whatever oversight he's discovered.

Jeff answers slowly, "Well, what are we going to say when he asks, 'And just how is all this stuff supposed to help me get back my bonus?'"

He's right. I'd overlooked this one. We think silently for a minute, but then I say, "You know what? If we get far enough to even hear this question, I think we'll already be well on our way to a win. So you know what I think we should do?"

Jeff is already nodding, "Not cross that bridge until we come to it?"

"Yep," I reply. "And look before we leap."

"And keep rolling so we gather no moss?"

"And because a moving target is harder to hit."

We're both smiling again. "I guess," Jeff says softly, "We're as ready as we'll ever be."

I nod, thinking what a lovely word "we" can be.

CHAPTER 9

There are risks and costs to a program of action. But they are far less than the long-range risks and costs of comfortable inaction."
—John F. Kennedy

THE NEXT MORNING I'M not surprised to feel butterflies in my stomach, but that doesn't mean I welcome them. I hate feeling nervous, although I've heard that some actors and athletes and other high-performance types welcome this feeling—they believe it gives them some beneficial edge. This is not for me. I'd rather feel relaxed and able to focus than wrestle with this skidding-along-ice, almost-out-of-control feeling.

I'm able to dissipate some of the nervousness with my morning run, as my mind works through all of the different scenarios I've played out in my "rehearsals" with Jeff and Keith over the last forty-eight hours. By the time I've finished my shower, I don't know whether I'm truly ready, but at least I'm confident I've done all I can.

I choose my most severe "power suit" for the day, feeling the need for a little extra corporate armor, and Keith nods his approval when I come downstairs. "Very strong," he commends as I take a bite of a muffin and a quick sip of coffee. As I move toward the door he takes me by the shoulders and says, "I'm not going to wish you luck, because you don't need any. You're ready. You're gonna stay focused and you're gonna remember why you're there and it will all be okay. You're gonna be fine."

He kisses my forehead more in benediction than in romance, and then turns me by my shoulders and gently nudges me toward the door. I smile at this gesture which we've used to send our kids to school more times than I can count, and when I glance back at him, he's smiling too.

I'm ready.

The butterflies return when I pull into the parking lot, and I try my best to dismiss them through sheer concentration. Competence, commitment, courage, compassion. I repeat these to myself as a kind of mantra. These are my tools. Competence, commitment, courage, compassion.

I make it through the shift-change meeting mostly on auto-pilot. My prized veteran, Roger, cracks wise about my suit, saying I must have a job interview on the outside. I give a generic smile and continue without responding, and later he catches me off to the side to say, "You're gonna be okay, kiddo," giving my arm a brief, reassuring squeeze.

I wonder how much he knows, reflecting on the small-town, everyone-knows-everything-about-everyone nature of most businesses, but I quickly decide to receive his gift of encouragement in the spirit he intended. Our person-states change with our interpretation of things, how we receive what's given—Roger didn't intend to make me suspicious of company gossip. He intended to enhance my sense of belongingness, and after I allow it, I find he has succeeded, warming me and easing my butterflies. I smile, and thank him, and make my way back to the admin building.

BEFORE I KNOW IT, it's time to meet Jeff in the lobby. He's waiting by the elevators; we make small talk and weak attempts at jokes as we ride up. No last-second strategy, no nervous double-checking—we both know it's too late for that. We're either ready or we're not.

We make our way down the hall-of-semi-fame to Barbara's desk, and while I doubt it's possible to surprise her, her eyes do open a fraction wider at the sight of Jeff and me together. No doubt she knows of her boss's separate meeting with Jeff, and she's probably aware of Pillar's plan to pit him against me, but she remains professionally cool as I greet her with, "Hi, Barbara—is he ready for us?"

She answers smoothly, "Good morning, Joanne—he's ready to see you, but I wasn't aware both of you would be meeting with him, so if you could just give me a moment—"

"No need for that," I say breezily, striding past her with Jeff behind me. "If he's ready, we'll just go on in! Thanks, Barbara." I don't bother looking back. I know her eyes will be icy at my having trumped her this way, and it's possible I've made an enemy, but our plan must be swift and surefooted, no time for half-measures. "All in," as they say in poker.

As I enter the office, I have a strong feeling of déjà vu, the past colliding with the present. I was just here a few days ago, and that time I had walked in as one woman and walked out a wreck of my former self. This time, I am coming in somewhat re-assembled, but I feel the way a ship's captain must feel when he studies his charts and realizes he must once again navigate the very reef on which he lost his last vessel.

I hear the door close behind us, and I feel a wave of comfort knowing that Jeff is here, too. The sound of the latch brings Pillar's eyes momentarily up from his computer monitor, and I'm sure they widen slightly before returning to their former, focused, too-busy-to-worry-about-you gaze.

"Jeff," he says shortly. "I didn't expect you to be a part of this."

"I know, sir, and I hope you don't mind," says Jeff in his most earnest, subordinate voice, "But after the work Joanne and I have been doing, we thought it would be more efficient for all of us to meet at once."

"Mmmm," mutters Pillar, his eyes again fixed on his monitor. "We'll sort that out in a minute or two. In the meantime, Joanne, I assume you've got some sort of progress to report?"

"Indeed I do sir," I say, and then I settle in to wait.

After only a moment or two, Pillar glances my way with irritation, "If you're trying to build suspense, I can assure you it isn't working." Again, he studies his monitor. "I've got a great deal to do and I'd appreciate it if you could get on with things, please."

"Yes, sir," I say, "I'm sure you would."

Again I wait, and again he breaks from his monitor and now the irritation is plainly audible in his voice as he glares at me, "Well then?"

"That's better, sir, thank you," I say smoothly.

His brow furrows, "For what?"

"For giving me your full attention. For behaving as though I'm a real live human being who has something important to say to you."

Pillar looks as though he's come home to find a nine-year-old painting his kitchen. "What the hell are you talking about?"

"I'm talking about the fact that when a coworker is speaking to you, she deserves respect—at bare minimum, she deserves your eye contact. When you stare at your monitor while I'm talking, I feel as though I might not have your full attention."

He leans forward, a predatory gleam in his eye, "Did it occur to you that perhaps I'm capable of doing two things at once?"

"Yes sir, of course it did," I answer promptly, "But I don't think anyone can do two things at once when one of them is to treat the person in front of you with respect, sir."

He glances to Jeff, perhaps wondering whether he should expect a flank attack before he returns to me, his voice filled with menace. "You have been tasked with addressing the shambles you've made of our safety program, and I don't think criticizing my degree of respect enters into things."

"Actually, sir, you'd be surprised about that," Jeff pipes up, and Pillar turns sharply to him. Jeff continues in a cheery voice, "We've made quite a few discoveries over the last few days and most of them connect to the fundamental culture of our workplace."

"Of which respect is an important part," I quickly add.

Pillar rolls his eyes and leans back in his chair, "Oh boy, here we go with the touchy-feely stuff, suddenly anything bad that happens anywhere in the world is nothing more than a problem of 'culture.' Have you two seriously come in here to tell me you've both swallowed the Culture Kool-Aid, the flavor of the month? Do you know how many newsletters and brochures and fliers I get offering to take a few thousand of this company's dollars in exchange for addressing our 'culture'? Please tell me you haven't spent the last week deciding to bring me 'culture' because I really don't have the time."

"And that, sir, is a perfect example of what we're talking about," I pounce.

Jeff moves in smoothly, "I know it may feel like an empty buzzword, sir, but 'culture' really is the best word to describe what we're talking about, which reflects the way a company performs and how the workers' attitudes and behaviors contribute to that performance."

"And just now," I pick up immediately, "the company's General Manager told two of his most important drivers of company performance he doesn't have time to hear the ideas they've spent the past week putting together. Does that sound like a company you'd like to work for?"

"We're not here to talk about whether this is a place I'd like to work; I already work here! We're here to talk about safety!" Pillar's face is darkening.

Jeff moves on, undaunted, "Yes sir, we're here to talk about safety—and part of what we've learned, Joanne and I, is that you can't talk about safety in a vacuum, it can't be addressed as though it's independent of other factors, that's the advantage of a culture-wide point of view, it allows us to—"

"Stop talking about culture!" Pillar thunders. "If you care to be specific with me, that's fine, but I won't sit here and listen to vague generalities being fobbed off as though they were deeply meaningful insights. That crap makes me sick!"

"Very well, sir," I say, making sure to keep my voice soft. "You're asking for specifics. I'll be happy to provide them. At this company, the General Manager asked the Director of Quality to compile a list of reasons justifying the dismissal of the Safety Director. At this company—"

Pillar is obviously taken aback by this, "What have you been telling her, Jeff?" But Jeff says nothing and I forge ahead.

"At this company, there's been a quantifiable improvement in safety, but senior management is more concerned with performance bonuses than with an injured employee whose injury may affect those bonuses. At this company, we—"

"Now wait a damned minute!" Pillar has his hand up in a "stop" gesture. "Just hold on, how can you say that?"

"How can I say what, sir?" I ask.

"How can you say we care more about bonuses than injuries?"

"Oh, I'm sorry, sir," I feign confusion. "Perhaps I misunderstood; I was under the impression from our last meeting the loss of your bonuses was your main concern and you viewed the injury as an irritation rather than a distressing and painful event that harmed one of your employees."

Pillar shakes his head, looking incredulous, "That's insane! Look, of course we care about mister, mister, you know—the fellow, down there, and his hand— of course we—"

"Sloan," I say quietly. "The injured worker's name is Doug Sloan."

Pillar is almost a hundred percent defensive at this point, and I know we have to be careful or else we'll risk the chance to achieve something positive. "Oohhhh, so this is how you're gonna play it," he says, nodding grimly. "This is the story you're trying to create, the heartless boss who can't even remember the name of the injured employee. Do you have any idea how many people work

here, do you seriously expect me to remember every single name?"

"Of course not, sir," Jeff responds.

"THEN WHAT THE HELL IS THIS ABOUT?" Pillar glares at both of us, his face flushed. Time to go for broke.

"Mr. Pillar, please," I say, keeping my voice even and businesslike. "You've made a series of mistakes, and you're embarrassed and upset about that just as anyone else would be, and—"

His face is pure disbelief, "*I've* made mistakes??"

"Yes sir, you have," I continue smoothly "and I'll be happy to explain what I mean in a moment, but in the meantime you've attempted to shift your own sense of wrongdoing onto the most convenient target, which is also a mistake and deep down you know it and you're even a little ashamed of yourself about it, and that's another thing feeding this big angry persona you're trying so hard to maintain, and—"

He barks a loud laugh, and it's clear he's struggling to present the image of total, contemptuous scorn, and the energy behind this effort is all I need to see to know my points are scoring more deeply than I might have hoped. "Ms. Cruse, you are clearly in need of some sort of counseling from which you might find guidance for this bizarre psychobabble of which you're so enamored, but I'm afraid we have a business to run, and it will run much more smoothly the minute you're out of the picture, so if this is all you've come to say, I think we can wrap it—"

"No, sir." This flat, firm statement from Jeff turns Pillar's head as sharply as if he had heard a pistol shot. He gapes at Jeff, who continues, "I don't think Joanne is going to be leaving the picture, because to dismiss her would be the biggest of all the mistakes she's talking about, whereas listening to her might be the biggest favor you ever did yourself, sir."

They stare at each other for a count of three, and I decide to forge ahead. Maybe this is how we'll wear him down—tag-teaming him like hunting dogs keeping a bear at bay. "Sir, we have the answer you asked for. We know how to improve our safety performance, and it's going to be a big effort and it's going to be hugely successful, and you will get the lion's share of the credit for having been so courageous to implement such daring new thinking. But none of that will happen unless you calm down and allow the three of us to discuss it as colleagues instead of adversaries."

Sure enough, this has him on his heels. He was in full battle mode, then Jeff turned his head with an unexpected sting on his flank, and then I turned his head yet again with the promise of a reward and the solution to all his troubles.

This isn't how he's used to fights happening; in his world, a fight consists only of an adversary who must be crushed, and I'm offering him a world in which his adversary offers to save him and let him get all the credit.

Whatever else Bob Pillar might be, he's not a stupid man, and he understands that when hit with so many confusing events so quickly, it's best to take a step back and re-assess his ground. "Let me see if I understand you so far," he says, slowly. He's working toward twin purposes—he wants to re-establish his control, while also making sure he has an accurate picture of what's been presented to him.

He continues, "You're saying this company has a culture problem which is affecting safety and, one would assume, other aspects of the company as well."

"Correct," I say.

Pillar shoots me a quick glance and continues, "You're also saying that specifically the problems you allude to can be seen in such things as management's attitude toward bonuses, and that we seem to value our own economic status more than we value our workers. And," he says, overriding my half-spoken agreement, "you're saying you know how to fix all of this and your ideas can be implemented in such a way that this office will be commended for its forward thinking. Is that accurate?"

I look to Jeff, who nods and says, "Yes sir, I'd say that's about it."

Pillar then asks, in an overly cordial voice, "Would it be appropriate at this time if I gave you a few preliminary thoughts on these topics?"

Uh-oh, I think, but what do you say when your boss asks whether you'll let him speak. "Of course," I say.

"The overarching thought I have upon hearing what you've said so far is essentially this: Get Bent."

"Sir," Jeff begins, but Pillar cuts him off.

"Do you really think I care about whether this office gets credit for this program or for that idea? Do you actually believe I can be manipulated by the promise of fame and glory? Let me make something clear for both of you—this office is judged based on the overall performance of the plant. That's it. Not for cute programs or daring ideas. Results. Do we make more than we spend? Are we able to retain our employees and our intellectual property? Are we in compliance with all regulations? That's it. The end. Simple. I don't care about credit, I care about results!"

He takes a moment to make sure this point has sunk home before continuing. "Now," he says, "If you have an idea, a specific idea, for how to improve our overall performance as a company, I'm all ears. If not, then please stop wasting my time."

There's a pause, which I eventually break. "Sir, if we've offended you with the way in which we tried to get your attention, I sincerely apologize. Things were getting emotional and it didn't seem as though you were in the mood to really listen."

Pillar spreads his arms, "I'm here, aren't I?"

I nod slowly, "Yes sir, but you were yelling, and you seemed to be feeling hostile to—"

"Oh, please!" He waves his hand dismissively, "When the heat is on, people tend to get heated, it's natural, and I have to say, it's not always a bad motivator to let people see you're upset, why, when I was in the army—"

"Motivator for what, sir?" Jeff asks quietly.

Pillar looks to him, "I'm sorry?"

"I asked, motivator for what?" Jeff leans in, his face intent, "If I understand you correctly, you're suggesting that letting your employees see you angry is a motivational ploy, like those used in sports or in the military, isn't that what you're saying?"

Pillar nods, defiant, "Exactly right, and I think history would show I'm correct."

"Yes sir," says Jeff, continuing, "But again, the question is, what is it that's being motivated? It sounds like negative reinforcement, meaning it teaches recipients they'll be better off if they avoid making you angry in the future, is that right?"

Pillar beams, "You got it."

"And may I ask, sir, how do they do that?"

Pillar is off balance at the apparent simplicity of the question. "Why, by doing their jobs properly, of course."

Jeff nods, "Yes sir. But is that the only tactic available to them?"

Pillar is obviously confused, "I don't understand what you're asking me."

"He's saying, sir, can't they also avoid your anger by simply avoiding you?" I ask. "This isn't a fifteen-man baseball team or a single platoon of soldiers. This is a big company, you just said yourself—hundreds of employees. Do they all have to shine at their jobs to avoid your anger, or couldn't they merely do everything possible to stay out of your way?"

Jeff leans in eagerly, "Remember when we lost Zytech as a customer last year?"

Pillar snorts, "Of course I do. That was a disaster."

"May I ask if you remember the cause, sir?"

Pillar shrugs, "Something to do with bad inspections. We tried to fire the guys who screwed it up but that turned into a union hassle."

Jeff is nodding, "Yes sir, and the reason it was a union hassle is that the inspectors themselves weren't the problem at all. It turned out we hadn't given them the tools they needed to do their inspections properly."

"Well sure, I know that's what they said in their hearing, but—"

"It was true, sir." Jeff's voice is quiet but firm. "All of us in Quality learned a lot from that episode. You see, sir, they had known for some time they lacked the tools necessary to do the job right, but they hadn't bothered mentioning it."

Pillar's face is startled, "Why in heaven's name not?"

My turn: "Because they felt they'd simply be yelled at, and they wanted to avoid your wrath." Pillar stares at me, and I continue, "You see, sir, your techniques had motivated them. They were motivated to keep a problem hidden, because fear of your anger was greater than their desire to do a good job. In their opinion, they felt the risk of speaking up outweighed the possible reward, so they kept quiet."

"And that, sir, is culture," Jeff concludes.

I let the silence expand for a moment. Time for compassion. "Sir," I say softly, "I don't believe for one instant you want anything but the best for this company. I think you've been doing the things you believe in your heart will generate the best results, the best performance, the best outcome. I think your intentions are straightforward and good, and you have the company's interests at heart every minute of the day."

"Do you?" he asks, obviously troubled by what he's been hearing.

"Yes sir, I do," I nod vigorously.

"But your employees can't see your intentions, sir," Jeff continues, "All they see is behavior. When your intention is motivation, they see anger. When your intention is to project an air of professionalism, they see coldness. When your intention is to make your company more competitive, you make it more cautious. You want your workers to be courageous, and speak up when they see a problem or a way to improve a process, but the culture around here doesn't facilitate that. Few people were ever taught to be brave by frightening them."

There's another lengthy silence, and this time I let it linger. Let's see what he'll say. After a time, he points to two pictures I never noticed behind his desk. They're pictures of Pillar, a pretty woman, and a handsome young man. "Do you know what my son said to me just last weekend?"

I'm intrigued; I never even knew Pillar had a son. He continues, "He said to me, 'Dad, is there anyone at the plant who loves that place half as much as you do?' And before I could even answer him, his mom said, 'Not a chance!' and then they both laughed."

He nods to himself, "Around my house, they believe the only thing I love more than them is this job. This place…" his voice trails for a moment, and I have the fleeting idea he's struggling with some powerful emotion. He returns to us, "And you know what? They're right. But apparently, I've been doing a pretty poor job of showing it."

"It's not just you, sir," Jeff begins, "You started working here at a time when management philosophies were very different, it certainly isn't your fault if—"

Pillar waves this away. "I don't care about that. Didn't you hear me earlier? My job is fundamental. You're saying we have a problem, and you've made your argument. I see your point. Perhaps it's time for some things to change."

Jeff and I look at each other—Is this really happening?

Pillar breaks into our moment of disbelief, "I was under the impression you had some sort of plan?"

Momentarily flustered, we begin laying out our documents. Jeff continues arranging them while I speak. "Sir, you may remember asking why we bothered with Behavior-Based Safety if it wasn't the best answer to our needs. In the past week Jeff and I have learned the BBS consultants had misled us into believing behavior is the genesis—the cause—of most injuries. Now we know this isn't true.

We've learned that, while behaviors are certainly important to notice and change when they are at-risk, but they are themselves the outcomes of pre-existing environmental conditions and person-states which we can, to a certain extent, influence, in turn improving behavior and company performance. Two days ago we attended a lecture by Dr. B.F. Pitz, who described what he calls the five critical person-states…"

Pillar listens carefully as we take turns explaining the basis of Actively Caring for People leadership. We point out the ways in which management practices in every department could be re-tooled to help maximize all five person-states, thereby providing every employee with a greater sense of commitment and ownership for the entire manufacturing process. Pillar listens attentively, taking notes and asking more than a few very astute questions. Some we can answer; others we hadn't considered, but he seems content to simply note them as points for further discussion.

At one point, Barbara interrupts to tell Pillar he's behind schedule and his appointments are starting to pile up. Pillar dismisses her curtly, telling her to reschedule whenever possible while asking the others to forgive him and indulge him a bit longer. As she is about to leave, obviously flustered, Pillar stops her.

"Barbara?" he calls, and she turns, pen at the ready to jot another command. But he simply says, "I know this is making a mess of things. I appreciate you doing your best to sort it out for me."

I thought "surprise" was the one expression I would never see on that woman's face…but apparently today is a day for exceptions. She manages a smile and then leaves, sending a quick glance our way, clearly wondering what we've done with her boss.

Pillar stands, and we reflexively do the same. "I'm going to want us to get all of this a bit more organized, and then I'd like the two of you to join me so we can present all of this to our senior management team, along with a specific timetable for implementation. Do you think you could have something ready in, say, two weeks?"

Jeff and I look at one another quickly. He nods and I say, "Absolutely." After a half beat I ask, "May I take it, sir, you'd like me to stay on to help with this new project?"

He looks at me evenly for a beat and then says, "Not if you're just gonna stand in here lolly-gagging. Get busy!"

Some things never change. We scramble to pick up our documents, and as we're hurrying out he calls from behind his desk, "Hey!"

We look up, alarmed, waiting. He looks at us both and then says simply, "Thank you."

And although Jeff still says he's not sure he saw it, I will go to my grave swearing that Bob Pillar winked at us before we turned to leave.

CHAPTER 10

"*If you want to lift yourself up, lift up someone else.*"
—**Booker T. Washington**

HI DOC! I CAN'T TELL YOU *how many times over the last few weeks I've sat down with every intention of beginning this letter, only to have something else pop up that needed my attention right away. We've been busier than I would have believed possible, but it has paid off with results I can only call astonishing—and it's all because of the profound lessons you and your work offer us.*

A lot has happened since we sat in the audience at your lecture six months ago. You know, it struck me that you changed my life twenty-five years ago when I was your student, and then you did it again at that lecture, and when we spoke afterward. You seem to make a habit of improving me every quarter century or so!

You probably remember what a mess I was that day—maybe not on the outside, but inside I was a disaster—filled with dread about my work and my future and about my very competence as a human being. You gave me back to myself, and helped me begin what feels like a brand new life—a life devoted to serving others through compassionate courage.

If the change in me is a blessing, then the change in our company has been an outright miracle. Practically everything about our culture has shifted for the better, and anyone who has been here for at least six months can see and feel the changes. Six months ago we did what was required and rarely went beyond the call of duty; now we work together to create and maintain a community of actively-caring-for-people individuals, all believing everyone is important and valued.

Of course this is worth achieving for its own sake, but the impact on our company's performance has been a nice bonus. Our outcome numbers are quite literally off the charts—we had to design new forms in order to keep track of our record-breaking results! Our employees are safer, our customers are happier, and our profits are making even Bob Pillar smile! Our various managers' debate the sources of this prosperity, but I just smile and think of you and your deceptively simple words, "It's all about Actively Caring for People."

Every source of my education—professors, books, consultants, colleagues—says a culture change takes years. I guess they'll have to write some new books, because we've shown it can happen in only a fraction of that time. Once Jeff and I had processed your ideas and succeeded in getting Mr. Pillar to listen to them, the changes were fast and furious. Pillar had us present our plans to our senior management team, and the buy-in was total and enthusiastic. They all showed courage by being open to feedback from everyone. Then they displayed more courage by owning up to their mistakes and correcting their behavior accordingly.

Things began to improve almost immediately, and have continued at a dizzying pace. I don't want to jinx us, but the fact is I see no reason for this progress to ever truly stop. I don't think it's possible to "max out" actively caring for people.

Even up in Corporate they don't quite know what to make of us, but they're going to learn. A short time ago they flew Mr. Pillar to Boston because they said they wanted "to learn more about this miracle we keep hearing about." They listened to his presentation and then did an unscheduled half hour or so of Q&A, and when they were done, they presented him with the President's Award for innovation. (They also quietly reinstated the bonuses which had been suspended, which didn't hurt!)

Before he left, they set up a return trip on which he and his team (meaning yours truly and Jeff!) will help them work out a plan for implementing the same techniques throughout all of our sister companies. We're a revolution!

When Mr. Pillar got back, he called the whole staff together, and presented the President's Award to everyone at the plant, saying we all earned it and thus it belongs to all of us. It's hanging in the company's main entrance now—it's the first thing we see every day when we arrive at work.

Throughout all of this, I've wondered from time to time, "What is culture?" And you know what I've decided? I'm convinced consultants make this culture stuff seem more complex than it really is. Our "culture" today is nothing more than us—people. People working together to achieve mutual goals for mutual benefit. Our dramatic success is due to each of us choosing, one by one, to help each other be the best we can be. We take care of each other. We have a brother/sister keeper's culture.

I think I now understand the real meaning of Gandhi's words, "Be the change you want to see." Living with an actively-caring-for-people mindset is what it's all about. Serving others is the best way to serve ourselves. And you did it, Doc—you started this transformation. You cared actively, and you showed me how to Be the Change You Want. You're the real deal.

Please stay well, and keep on working your magic. The world needs you.

God bless and much love,

Joanne

P.S. Please find enclosed a special green wristband. All our employees are wearing these with pride. I think the four words on the wristband say it all: "Actively Caring for People." We like when people get curious and ask us what it means. We explain what AC4P is and we give a couple of examples, and then I tell them it all started with you...and it can continue through them.

They like the sound of that. XO J

EPILOGUE

We wrote this storybook to teach the courage and compassion of "actively caring for people" (AC4P) leadership. We believe our world will be a better place when each of us does a little more to help others. Perhaps the best way to change a culture and offset the distress and destruction of a fast-paced world growing in terrorism is to promote interdependency and a win-win community spirit through AC4P behavior. When we serve others, we benefit ourselves as well. Our own self-esteem, self-efficacy, personal control, optimism and sense of belongingness increase when we choose to act responsibly and go beyond the call of duty for other people.

Some might say the examples in this book are too unbelievable and over the top. In fact, we have experienced each of these stories to be true on more than one occasion and in more than one situation. In fact, we're sure most readers will attest to this.

We invite you to do any or all of the following:

1. *Notice your own behavior daily.* Ask yourself the question, "Did I actively care for someone today?" Please send us some real-world examples of your AC4P behaviors and outcomes, and let us know if we can share your story with others. Your anecdote could be the very exemplar that inspires compassionate courage from another person.

2. *Send us your stories* about what works or doesn't work to increase AC4P behavior among others. What have you noticed around your workplace that facilitates or hinders the courage and/or compassion needed for genuine actively caring?

3. *Tell us how you felt* before and after your own AC4P behavior. Did you experience a boost in any of the five critical person-states: self-esteem, belongingness, self-efficacy, personal control, and optimism? Which ones?

We would love to hear how your AC4P behavior influenced the five person-states, or perhaps had another benefit we haven't discussed in this book. Although the AC4P principles presented here are evidence-based, the empirical research on real-world application is limited. We have much to learn. Your stories and testimonies can help us move forward on developing a more AC4P society. We envision a follow-up book that reports readers' testimonies regarding confirmation versus disconfirmation of the life principles presented in *The Courage to Actively Care*.

For those in the safety world, we hope you see beyond the observation and feedback process of behavior-based safety (BBS) into the deeper human dynamics affected by contributing interpersonal service to others. Many companies measure progress in BBS by the number of observations conducted or the number of people observed. This can be a misleading measure of BBS success. A more valid indicator of safety success is the number of people conducting behavior-based observation and feedback sessions with compassionate AC4P courage. Concern with people's attitudes and person-states during a behavior-based coaching session reflects an evolution from BBS to AC4P Safety.

The power of PBS is in the development of a community of caring. A brother/sister keeper's culture is achieved when people look out for each other and support an AC4P spirit. AC4P Safety represents not only an evolution from BBS, but also an expansion beyond safety into all other domains of life.

We acknowledge the late Joel Henning for his wisdom in suggesting in *The Future of Staff Groups* that all functions of an organization are only worth personal investment when they systematically impact a greater whole beyond a narrow target subject or functional area. We believe safety is a specialty, poised to not only prevent injuries but also to cultivate a spirit of AC4P and servant leadership throughout a culture. This is the courage and compassion of the AC4P approach to improving the effectiveness of individuals, groups, organizations, and communities. We look forward to receiving personal testimonies that support this premise.

Please mail your personal stories to: Make-A-Difference, LLC, P.O. Box 73, Newport, VA 24128-0073. Or e-mail your inputs to the authors at: esgeller@vt.edu and organizationaleffectiveness@msn.com.

*For more information on AC4P safety, including relevant books and education/training materials, log onto www.safetyperformance.com. Plus, learn more about the AC4P Movement at www.ac4p.org

DISCUSSION QUESTIONS
FOR PERSONAL APPLICATION

CHAPTER 1

1. Have you ever participated in a behavior-based safety (BBS) observation and feedback process; and if so, what barriers hindered its progress?

2. Describe your personal reaction to an injury to one of your peers. What factors were presumed to contribute to that incident, and how were they addressed?

3. At times someone gets injured because of an at-risk behavior which occurs because the person is trying to do the right thing within the context of the management system. Did you ever perform an at-risk behavior because of a system-encouraged decision? Explain.

4. How do you get beyond the common emphasis of productivity over safety?

5. How do you celebrate safety results? What kinds of results do you celebrate?

CHAPTER 2

1. To what extent do high-tech communication methods like email or voicemail stifle effective conversation and/or the development of healthy relationships?

2. Have you ever had an encounter with a boss or supervisor analogous to the exchange between Joanne Cruse and Bob Pillar? How did it make you feel? How did that situation impact your subsequent contribution to the company?

3. Do you feel personal ownership of safety in your organization? What would it take to get more employees engaged in organizational efforts to prevent injuries?

4. Do incentives or rewards motivate you to work safely? What kind of safety incentives and rewards work best for injury reduction, ones based on outcomes (i.e., injuries) or ones based on proactive behaviors and activities (i.e., what people do to prevent injuries)? Why?

CHAPTER 3

1. How has the support of a friend or peer enabled you to overcome a distressing or bothersome situation at work?

2. Why didn't Joanne stop to help the person with the flat tire? Can you remember a time when someone needed your help and you could have stopped to help but you didn't? How did that make you feel?

3. Consider a time when the comfort from a family member enabled you to deal with emotional turmoil. How did your family member attempt to help you recover, and why did this work or not?

4. Describe a time when an interpersonal interaction at work made it difficult for you to get to sleep.

5. What is empathy? What were the benefits of Keith's empathy for Joanne?

CHAPTER 4

1. Describe a time when you reached out to a colleague at work for critical advice or emotional support. How frequently or infrequently does this occur?

2. Does an emphasis on injury reports as a measure of safety motivate the cover-up of some injuries? If yes, explain why this occurs.

3. Explain how quality and safety are independent vs. integrated at your workplace with regard to measurement, management reviews, and financial incentives/rewards?

4. Do you believe behavior is a primary cause of most injuries and property damage? Explain.

5. When someone doesn't use a safety belt in your car, what do you do? Does this depend on whether the unbuckled passenger is a family member? Why?

6. How do you use information about close calls or near hits? When information on such close calls is collected and then distributed to all employees, does this result in discussions related to risk reduction and injury prevention?

7. What are your key safety metrics, and how frequently are they reviewed by you and your co-workers?

CHAPTER 5

1. Explain how Coach Casey's definition of courage (i.e., "love the game") relates to your behavior at work.

2. What behaviors are practiced by the best coaches? How does this apply to safety?

3. How does the scoring methods at a baseball game, from the scoreboard on the field to the recording of individual player statistics, relate to the measurement of your organization's performance?

4. Have you seen demonstrations of courage at your job site? Explain.

5. What does "compassion" mean to you, and how does compassion relate to courage?

6. Do you feel bad when you don't intervene to stop someone from performing an at-risk behavior? Why or why not?

7. What does it mean to perform in order to "avoid failure"? Explain the advantages and disadvantages of such an approach to your work.

CHAPTER 6

1. What holds people back from helping others in an emergency situation?
2. Define "actively caring for people" as it relates to a specific set of circumstances at your workplace.
3. Explain how "courage" contributes to "competence" and "commitment" in determining individual or organizational performance?
4. What is self-talk and what role does it play in your tendency to perform actively care for people (AC4P) behavior?
5. List the five person-states that influence a person's willingness to perform AC4P behavior, and describe how each of these states are lowered or raised by interpersonal situations at work.
6. Discuss specific ways to enhance the five person-states at your workplace.
7. How do you use storytelling to impact safety?

CHAPTER 7

1. Describe a time when your behavior was influenced by a dramatic change in one or more of the five AC4P person-states: self-esteem, self-efficacy, personal control, optimism, and belongingness.
2. Reflect on a time when you had an opportunity to actively care and you didn't. What held you back?
3. What can be done to increase a person's sense of belongingness in an organization?
4. Explain the advantages and disadvantages of a "cookie-cutter" approach to implementing a program designed to enhance organizational performance.
5. Describe two demonstrations of courage you have personally experienced, one with and one without compassion.
6. Do you believe everyone has the potential to act with compassion? Why or why not?
7. Offer some specific ways to potentially increase compassion in yourself and among others, at home and at work.

CHAPTER 8

1. Why is it wrong to assume most injuries are caused by behavior?
2. Describe a time when it took courage for you to confront another individual in order to solve a problem. What factors made this challenging, and how did you gain the courage needed to follow through with this encounter?
3. Describe a time when you experienced compassion in yourself or from another person during an interpersonal conversation.
4. What factors determine whether you confront issues with compassionate courage?
5. Explain the meaning of this statement: "Practice does not make perfect; only with behavior-based feedback can we improve."
6. Consider some important interpersonal conversations in your professional life, from interviewing for a job to giving or receiving a performance evaluation. How did you prepare for these conversations? Do you wish you had done more to prepare for any of these? Explain.
7. What is synergy? How do you get synergy with other employees in your organization?

CHAPTER 9

1. Consider a time when you felt "butterflies in your stomach" in anticipation of an upcoming event. Were the butterflies organized and all aligned (meaning you were prepared and in control) or were the butterflies disorganized and in disarray (meaning you were not prepared nor in control)?
2. What does the term "culture" mean to you, and how does it influence behavior and/or attitude?
3. Have you ever had a coworker treat you as an object or only a means to an end instead of an individual with feelings who contributes worthwhile work? Describe an interpersonal encounter with this person that contributed to your perception of being "mistreated."

4. When have you confronted an individual in a higher-ranking job than yours? What factors contributed to the positive vs. negative aspects of that interaction?

5. What does it mean to call something "flavor of the month," and what workplace conditions or interpersonal dynamics contribute to this label?

6. How do you build ownership for anything in an organization?

7. What qualities of effective leadership were displayed in the conversation between Joanne, Jeff, and Bob Pillar?

CHAPTER 10

1. Do you believe a work culture can change dramatically in only six months? Why or why not?

2. What factors can accelerate a culture change in an organization?

3. Consider individuals who have had a significant professional impact on your life. How did they do that? What were the effects on your five person-states?

4. In your opinion, which events of this entire story were realistic, and which were not?

5. Explain the meaning of Gandhi's words: "Be the change you want to see," perhaps by describing a personal experience.

6. Define the four key C-words of the story—competence, commitment, courage, and compassion—and explain why leaders need to display each of these qualities in order to be optimally effective.

7. Define specific ways you could increase the frequency and/or improve the effectiveness of AC4P behavior in your work culture.

BIBLIOGRAPHY AND RECOMMENDED READING

The AC4P principles and applications revealed in this book are supported by the following books and research-based journal articles.

Aronson, E. (1999). The power of self-persuasion. *American Psychologist, 54,* 875–884.

Bailey, J. S., & Burch, M. B. (2006). *How to think like a behavior analyst.* Mahwah, N.J.: Lawrence Erlbaum Associates.

Bandura, A. (1997). *Self-Efficacy: The exercise of control.* New York: W. H. Freeman and Company.

Bem, D. J. (1972). Self-perception theory. In L. Berkowitz (Ed.). *Advances in experimental social psychology*, Vol. 6 (pp. 1–60). New York: Academic Press.

Bennis, W. (1989). *On becoming a leader.* New York: Addison-Wesley Publishing Company.

Biglan, A. (2015). *The nurture effect: How the science of human behavior can improve our lives and our world.* Oakland, CA: New Harbinger Publications.

Bird, F. E., Jr., & Germain, G. L. (1987). *Commitment.* Loganville, GA: International Loss Control Institute, Inc.

Blanchard, K., Zigarmi, P., & Zigarmi, D. (1985). *Leadership and the one-minute manager.* New York: William Morrow and Company, Inc.

Block, P. (1993). *Stewardship*. San Francisco: Berrett-Koehler Publishers Inc.

Braksick, L. W. (2000). *Unlock behavior, Unleash profits*. New York: McGraw Hill.

Brehm, J. W. (1972). *Responses to loss of freedom: A theory of psychological reactance*. New York: General Learning Press.

Brown, J., & Isaacs, D. (2005). *The world café*. San Francisco: Berrett-Koehler Publishers, Inc.

Carnegie, D. (1936). *How to win friends and influence People* (1981 Edition). New York: Galahad Books.

Cialdini, R. B. (2001). *Influence: Science and practice* (4th ed.). New York: Harper Collins College.

Collins, J. C. (2001). *Good to great*. Harper Collins Publishers, Inc.

Collins, J. C., & Porras, J. (1994). *Built to last*. New York: HarperCollins Publishers, Inc.

Connolly, M., & Rianoshek, R. (2002). *The communication catalyst*. Dearborn, MI: Dearborn Trade Publishing.

Covey, S. R. (1989). *The seven habits of highly effective people: Restoring the character ethic*. New York: Simon & Schuster, Inc.

Covey, S. R. (2004). *The eighth habit: From effectiveness to greatness*. New York: Simon & Schuster, Inc.

Daniels, A. C., & Daniels, J. E. (2005). *Measure of a leader*. Atlanta, GA: Performance Management Publications.

Deci, E. L., & Flaste, R. (1995). *Why we do what we do: Understanding self-motivation*. New York: Penguin Books.

DeGeus, A. (1997). *The living company*. Cambridge, MA: Harvard Business School Press.

DePree, M. (1989). *Leadership is an art*. New York: Dell Publishing Group, Inc.

Deming, W. E. (1986). *Out of the crisis*. Cambridge, MA: Massachusetts Institute of Technology, Center for Advanced Engineering Study.

DePasquale, J. P., & Geller, E. S. (1999). Critical success factors for behavior-based safety: A study of 20 industry-wide applications. *Journal of Safety Research, 30*(4), 237–249.

Elder, J. P., Geller, E. S., Hovell, M. F., & Mayer, J. A. (1994). *Motivating health behavior.* New York: Delmar Publishers.

Festinger, L. (1957). *A theory of cognitive dissonance.* Stanford, CA: Stanford University Press.

Frankl, V. (1962). *Man's search for meaning: An introduction to logo therapy.* Boston: Beacon Press.

Geller, E. S. (1994). Ten principles for achieving a total safety culture. *Professional Safety, 39* (9), 18.

Geller, E. S. (1995). Safety coaching: Key to achieving a total safety culture. *Professional Safety, 40* (7), 16–22.

Geller, E. S. (1997). Key processes for continuous safety improvement: Behavior-based recognition and celebration. *Professional Safety, 42*(10), 40–44.

Geller, E. S. (1998). *Understanding behavior-based safety: Step-by-step methods to improve your workplace* (2nded.). Neenah, WI: J. J. Keller & Associates, Inc.

Geller, E. S. (1999). Behavior-based safety: Confusion, controversy, and clarification. *Occupational Health & Safety, 68*(1), pp. 40, 42, 44, 46, 48–49.

Geller, E. S. (2000). Behavioral safety analysis: A necessary precursor to corrective action. *Professional Safety, 45*(3), 29–32.

Geller, E. S. (2000). Ten leadership qualities for a total safety culture: Safety management is not enough. *Professional Safety, 45*(5), 38–41.

Geller, E. S. (2001). Actively caring for occupational safety: Extending the performance management paradigm. In C. M. Johnson, W.K. Redmon, & T.C. Mawhinney (Eds.). *Handbook of organizational performance: Behavior analysis and management* (pp.303-326). New York: The Haworth Press.

Geller, E. S. (2001). *Beyond safety accountability: How to increase personal responsibility.* Rockville, MD: Government Institutes.

Geller, E. S. (2001). *The psychology of safety handbook.* Boca Raton, FL: CRC Press.

Geller, E.S. (2016) (Ed.). *Applied psychology: Actively caring for people.* New York: Cambridge University Press.

Geller, E.S. (2016). Seven life lessons from humanistic behaviorism: How to bring the best out of yourself and others. *Journal of Organizational Behavior Management, 35*(1), 151-170.

Geller, E.S. (2017). *Actively caring for people in schools: How to cultivate a culture of compassion.* New York: Morgan James Publishers.

Geller, E. S., & Clarke, S. W. (1999). Safety self-management: A key behavior-based process for injury prevention. *Professional Safety, 44*(7), 29–33.

Geller, E.S., & Kipper, B. (2017). *Actively caring for people policing: Building positive police/citizen relations.* New York: Morgan James Publishers.

Geller, E. S., Roberts, D. S., & Gilmore, M. R. (1996). Predicting propensity to actively care for occupational safety. *Journal of Safety Research, 27*, 1–8.

Geller, E.S., & Veazie, B. (2014). Behavior-based safety versus actively caring: From other directed compliance to self-directed commitment. *Professional Safety, 59*(10), 44-50.

Geller, E.S., & Veazie, B. (2017). *The Motivation in Actively Care: How You Can Make it Happen.* New York: Morgan James Publishers.

Geller, E. S., & Williams, J. A. (2001) (Eds.). *Keys to behavior-based safety from Safety Performance Solutions.* Rockville, MD: Government Institutes.

Goleman, D. (1995). *Emotional intelligence.* New York: Bantam Books.

Henning, J. (1997). *The future of staff groups.* San Francisco: Berrett-Koehler Publishers, Inc.

Hersey, P., & Blanchard, K. (1982). *Management of organizational behavior* (4th ed.). Englewood Cliffs, NJ: Prentice Hall.

Holdsambeck, R.D., & Pennypacker, H.S. (2016) (Eds.). *Behavioral science: Tales of inspiration, discovery, and service.* Beverly, MA: The Cambridge Center for Behavioral Studies.

Katzenbach, J. (1995). *Real change leaders.* New York: Random House, Inc.

Kaye, B., & Jordan-Evans, S. (2002). *Love 'em or lose 'em: Getting good people to stay.* San Francisco: Berrett-Koehler Publishers, Inc.

Kirkpatrick, S. A., & Locke, E. A. (1991). Leadership: Do traits matter? *Academy of Management Executive, 5*(2), 48-60.

Kotter, J. P. (1996). *Leading change.* Boston, MA: Harvard Business School Press.

Kotter, J. P. (1999). *What leaders really do.* Boston, MA: Harvard Business School Press.

Kouzes, J. M., & Posner, B. Z. (2006). *A leader's legacy.* San Francisco : John Wiley & Sons, Inc.

Krisco, K. H. (1997). *Leadership and the art of conversation.* Rocklin, CA: Prima Publishing.

Langer, E. J. (1989). *Mindfulness.* Reading, MA: Addison-Wesley.

Langer, E. J. (1997). *The power of mindful learning.* Reading, MA: Perseus Books.

Latané, B., & Darley, J. M. (1970). *The unresponsible bystander: Why doesn't he help?* New York: Appleton-Century-Crofts.

Ludwig, T. D., & Geller, E. S. (2001). *Intervening to improve the safety of occupational driving: A behavior change model and review of empirical evidence.* New York: The Haworth Press, Inc.

Maslow, A. H. (1943). A theory of human motivation. *Psychological Review, 50,* 370-396.

Messick, D. M., & Kramer, R. M. (2005) (Ed.). *The psychology of leadership: New perspectives and research.* Mahwah, N.J.: Lawrence Erlbaum Associates.

McSween, T. E. (2001). *The values-based safety process: Improving your safety culture with behavior-based safety* (2nd ed.). Hoboken, NJ: John Wiley & Sons, Inc.

Petersen, D. (2001). *Authentic involvement.* Itasca, IL: National Safety Council.

Rotter, J. B. (1966). Generalized expectancies for internal versus external control of reinforcement. *Psychological Monographs, 80,* No. 1.

Ryan, R. M., & Deci, E. L. (2000). Self-determination theory and the facilitation of intrinsic motivation, social development, and well-being. *American Psychologist, 55,* 68–78.

Seligman, M. E. P. (1991). *Learned optimism.* New York: Alfred A. Knopf.

Senge, P. M. (1990). *The fifth discipline: The art and practice of the learning organization.* New York: Doubleday/Currency.

Senge, P., Kleiner, A., Roberts. C., Ross. R., Roth. G., & Smith, B. (1999). *The dance of change.* New York: Doubleday Publishing.

Skinner, B. F. (1971). *Beyond freedom and dignity.* New York: Knopf.

Skinner, B. F. (1981). Selection by consequences. *Science, 213*, 502.

The Arbinger Institute (2006). *Leadership and self-deception: Getting out of the box.* San Francisco: Berrett-Koehler Publishers, Inc.

Watson, D. L., & Tharp, R. G. (1997). *Self-directed behavior: Self-modification for personal adjustment* (7thed.). Pacific Grove, CA: Brooks/Cole.

Wheatley, M. (1999). *Leadership and the new science.* San Francisco: Berrett-Koehler Publishers, Inc.

ABOUT THE AUTHORS

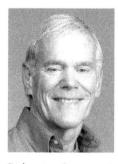 **E. Scott Geller**, Ph.D., an Alumni Distinguished Professor at Virginia Tech, is co-founder and senior partner of Safety Performance Solutions, Inc., a leading-edge training and consulting organization specializing in AC4P safety since 1995 (safetyperformance.com). For almost five decades, Professor Geller has taught and conducted research as a faculty member and director of the Center for Applied Behavior Systems in the Department of Psychology.

He has authored, edited or co-authored 27 books, 82 book chapters, 39 training programs, 259 magazine articles, and more than 300 research articles addressing the development and evaluation of behavior-change interventions to improve quality of life on a large scale. His most recent textbook: *Applied Psychology: Actively Caring for People* defines Dr. Geller's research, teaching, and scholarship career at Virginia Tech, which epitomizes the VT logo: *Ut Prosim—* "That I May Serve".

Dr. Geller is a Fellow of the American Psychological Association, the Association for Psychological Science, the Association of Behavior Analysis International, and the World Academy of Productivity and Quality Sciences.

He is past Editor of the *Journal of Applied Behavior Analysis* (1989-1992), current Associate Editor of *Environment and Behavior* (since 1982), and current Consulting Editor for *Behavior and Social Issues*, the *Journal of Organizational Behavior Management, and* the *Journal of Safety Research.*

Professor Geller has received lifetime achievement awards from the International Organizational Behavior Management Network (in 2008) and the American Psychological Foundation (in 2009). In 2010, he was honored with the Outstanding Applied Research Award from the American Psychological Association's Division of Applied Behavior Analysis. In 2011, the College of Wooster awarded E. Scott Geller the honorary degree: Doctor of Humane Letters.

Bob Veazie is President of People Powered Leadership (PPL) with a mission to help organizations develop high performance safety cultures through employee inclusion and empowerment. PPL's primary focus is to help organizations develop an injury-free safety culture utilizing a "Commitment-Based" approach. Bob has worked in industry for about 30 years at Shell Oil Company, Fluor Corporation and Hewlett Packard Company.

Bob Veazie has been a keynote speaker at numerous professional development conferences (ASSE, NSC, VPPPA, BSN, WEI, Alaska Governor's Conference, Industry Week Best Plants and more) and has authored articles in both *Professional Safety* and *Industrial Safety Hygiene News*. Bob has spoken at company management team meetings as well as presented the new paradigm on Commitment Based Safety to corporate leadership teams. Since forming his own safety consulting company eight years ago, Bob has worked with tens of thousands of employees in many diverse industries to apply behavioral solutions to managing risks and reducing injuries in organizations.

Bob earned his Bachelor of Science in Business Management from California Polytechnic State University at San Luis Obispo in 1978 and a Masters of Business Administration from California State University at Long Beach in 1981.

Bob has studied organizational performance with some of the top thought leaders in the field—Dr. Stephen Covey, Peter Senge, Peter Block, Margaret Wheatley, Ken Blanchard, David Whyte and many more, As well, Bob has worked and studied key psychological principles under the mentorship of Dr. E. Scott Geller including applications to reduce injuries in organizations.

ACKNOWLEDGMENTS

The Courage to Actively Care is a revision and re-publication of *The Courage Factor,* published in 2008 by Coastal Training Technologies Corp. and disseminated exclusively at select safety conferences. Bob Veazie and I are extremely grateful that David Hancock, CEO of Morgan James Publishers, perceived value in a wider distribution of this narrative approach to teaching principles and applications of psychological science relevant for promoting the Actively Caring for People (AC4P) Movement. We greatly appreciate the competent contributions of the Morgan James publication team led by Margo Toulouse. They prepared our scholarship for publication, from designing the cover to formatting the text and illustrations.

This realistic narrative brings to life the most practical and effective leadership principles included in the seventeen safety-related books I've authored or co-authored since 1996. Thus, this storybook has benefited from the cumulative advice, support and encouragement of literally hundreds of colleagues, teachers, students and safety leaders. My prior books thanked many of these individuals. Here, I recognize those with whom I've worked directly to accomplish this scholarship.

First and foremost, I'm profoundly grateful for the talent, dedication and inspiration of my co-author—Bob Veazie. I first met Bob in 1997 when he invited me to offer workshops to the management team and hourly workers at the Hewlett Packard (HP) facility in Corvallis, Oregon. As a Culture-Change Agent for the 6,000 employees at that plant, Bob exemplified "compassionate courage," a label that was not in my vocabulary at the time. He literally walked and talked safety throughout the facility, from commending employees for their injury-prevention actions to appealing to managers for additional safety-related support. Indeed, I had never met anyone who was so genuinely dedicated to occupational safety all day and every day.

Bob took the behavior-based principles I taught and customized practical procedures and accountability systems to enable the Corvallis HP facility to reach record-high levels of safety excellence. And most relevant to this book, Bob was the first practitioner to truly appreciate the innovative and practical potential of the "actively caring for people" (AC4P) dimension of my teaching.

Others have shown interest and appreciation for the notion that one's propensity to actively care—to go beyond the call of duty on behalf of another person's well-being—is influenced by certain person-states that vary as a function of interpersonal communication. However, Bob made these assumptions behavior-based, and recorded instances that supported their validity.

This storybook was Bob Veazie's idea. Convinced of the potency and practical potential of the AC4P concepts and proposals he had learned from my workshops and books, Bob enticed me to collaborate on this challenging venture—the creation of a fun-to-read book that brings to life the essential leadership lessons anyone can use to improve behavior, attitude and organizational performance.

Bob outlined a storyline, and then asked me to link principles with practical applications. We deemed it necessary to use real-world characters and incidents to illustrate lessons and implementations. Bob's experiences at HP were invaluable, as well as my own interactions in the business world. However, one particular safety professional sparked our rhetoric about courage and compassion: Joanne Dean, the Safety Director of the Gale Construction Company, a subsidiary of Mack-Cali.

I met Joanne at a safety conference fifteen years ago, and ever since, I've been impressed with this individual's daily dedication to preventing injuries among hundreds of construction workers and company leaders. I reported her remarkable AC4P behavior in several of my monthly "Psychology of Safety" columns in *Industrial Safety and Hygiene News*. For example, she helped to develop a large consortium of safety leaders from major construction firms throughout New Jersey who meet monthly to share leading-edge strategies and accountability systems for injury prevention; she arranged for the high-school classmates of a victim of ALS (Lou Gehrig's disease) to document their compassion and caring for this talented athlete, coach and community leader in a memorable and heart-warming book; she taught emergency medical response skills to company employees throughout New Jersey; she consistently exemplifies the principles and procedures of AC4P in group meetings and in one-on-one conversations; and as a professional health and fitness instructor for more than 45 years, Joanne has guided and motivated the integration of health-enhancing exercise into the lifestyles of countless individuals. But most notably, Joanne Dean never fails to step to the plate for occupational safety, even when such action puts her at risk for an uncomfortable interaction. Joanne rarely fails at these interpersonal interventions because her courage is always compassionate; she actively cares for people.

Joanne Dean epitomizes the four key leadership concepts illustrated in this book—competence, commitment, courage, and compassion. Her special success as a safety leader verifies the social and societal validity of the life lessons portrayed here. Thus, it's fitting that we dedicated our story to Joanne Dean, and named the lead character "Joanne."

The name of another key character in our story was purposely assigned Dr. Pitz, the distinguished professor who teaches Joanne critical leadership lessons that change her life. Dr. Gordon F. Pitz was the chair of both my thesis and dissertation committees in graduate school at Southern Illinois University (SIU) in Carbondale, Illinois. He gave me special coaching in research methodology and data analysis, and refined my skills for professional writing. Most importantly, Dr. Pitz became my mentor at a critical time in my graduate education.

My first year in graduate school, I was assigned to work in the animal research laboratory of a professor with whom I did not get along. He told me I lacked the ability and dedication to become a successful researcher, while I perceived him to be a disorganized individual, more interested in personal fame than teaching.

This assistant professor convinced his research staff I should not be in graduate school, and he spread this perspective to other students and faculty.

With low self-esteem, self-efficacy, personal control, optimism and belongingness in my assigned research environment, I was on the verge of quitting graduate school at the end of my first year. Fortunately, I met Dr. Pitz in the midst of my darkest time since leaving home for my undergraduate education. This professor overlooked the negative talk about my research performance, and awarded me a graduate research assistantship to work in his human information processing and decision-making laboratory. This was a courageous act for a non-tenured, assistant professor. But Dr. Pitz did much more; he actively cared for my successive development as a researcher, teacher and scholar. He helped me recharge those five person-states that had been depleted throughout my first year at SIU, and thereby enabled me to feel competent and committed throughout the remaining four years of my graduate education.

My career as an author of books for the business world has benefited greatly from the talent and insight of Dave Johnson, Editor of *Industrial Safety and Hygiene News*. As a friend and professional colleague since 1999, Dave has taught me how to translate academic theory and research into concise language suitable for public consumption. Dave was the editor of four of my occupational safety books, and my co-author for *People-Based Patient Safety*, a comprehensive treatise of evidence-based and practical methods for preventing human error in healthcare settings.

We were privileged to engage the special skills and talents of Bo Wilson, a highly acclaimed author and playwright. Bo Wilson's artful treatment of our draft chapters distinguishes this book from all other storybooks prepared for human development, organizational enhancement, and/or culture enrichment. More specifically, Bo's prudent modifications of our written expression add vivid reality to the cast of our story and to their various teaching/learning episodes.

Bo's dramatic refinement of our scholarship involved much more than editing. He not only substituted words and sentences to develop our story characters and add drama, he eliminated substantial text that was unnecessary and distracting, and then made significant additions, enhancing realism and incorporating humor. We could not have turned our drafts over to a better-equipped artist. Thank you, Bo Wilson, for making our book the most true-to-life and fun-to-read among the countless other self-help and human development storybooks on the market.

How did we find and employ Bo Wilson? Nancy Kondas made this happen. Indeed, Nancy Kondas has been key to the development, production, and marketing of each of my four books published by Coastal Training Technologies Corp. From the initiation of a book plan to the final review of page proofs, I relied on the advice, acumen, vision and supportive management of Nancy Kondas. I'm convinced none of my People-Based Safety books would have seen the light of day without the dedication and leadership of this VP of Creative Product Development for Coastal Training Technologies. Bob and I are indebted to Nancy Kondas for the expected success of this book to make a difference in people's lives. Words are insufficient to express our utmost gratitude. Thank you, Nancy!

Also, I am extremely appreciative for the unique and unvarying support of Ashley Underwood and Brian Doyle, the current Coordinators of Virginia Tech's Center for Applied Behavior Systems which I direct. Not only did Ashley and Brian assume critical leadership roles that enabled me to work on this revision, they prepared the text and illustrations for the publisher.

This brings me to two additional noteworthy contributors to this book—Marshall McClure and George Wills. Marshall McClure applied her creativity and composition skills to qualify our first edition (*The Courage Factor*) for printing. This included the formatting of original artwork by George Wills, a professional illustrator from Blacksburg, Virginia. George has supported my teaching with his imaginative artwork for more than 25 years. Since 1990, I have used George's original cartoons, created and customized per my instructions, to illustrate concepts in my university classes and to add humor in my keynote addresses. Indeed, all of my safety and leadership books have been enhanced with George Wills' artistic talents; this book is no exception.

George's illustrations interspersed throughout this book depict his interpretation of our story characters in various situations. We think they add vitality and drama to the printed prose, and thereby enhance readability. We hope you feel the same.

Any book project is a collaborative team effort, and I have identified only the key players here. Many others contributed to this product, including hundreds of colleagues who have provided Bob Veazie and me the teaching/learning experiences and revelations reflected in our story. The synergy from your interdependent support and sustenance bestows a noble legacy—leadership lessons and applications readers can use to improve interpersonal relationships, enhance individual, group and organizational performance, and enrich a culture.

E. Scott Geller

OTHER AC4P BOOKS BY E. SCOTT GELLER

Morgan James
Speakers Group

www.TheMorganJamesSpeakersGroup.com

We connect Morgan James published authors with live and online events and audiences whom will benefit from their expertise.

Printed in the USA
CPSIA information can be obtained
at www.ICGtesting.com
JSHW082341140824
68134JS00020B/1815